OUR STRUGGLE WITH
Good & **EVIL**

Dr. Roberto Estevez

OUR STRUGGLE WITH GOOD AND EVIL
By: Dr. Roberto Estevez

Published by
GOSPEL FOLIO PRESS
304 Killaly St. W.
Port Colborne, ON L3K 6A6
CANADA

ISBN: 9781927521410

Cover design by Danielle Elzinga

All Scripture quotations from the
King James Version unless otherwise noted.

Printed in USA

OUR STRUGGLE WITH
Good & **EVIL**

Contents

Acknowledgments

I want to thank my brother and fellow author, Ricardo Estevez of Uruguay, for his valuable collaboration and helpful corrections and insights.

Dr. James Bartley (former director of the Baptist Seminary of Uruguay) for his commentary, enthusiasm, and encouragement in the development of this book.

Dr. Jim Haesemeyer for his excellent work as a translator and editor.

B. W. Hopkins, Th.D. (Former Vice President, Dean, and Professor Emeritus Moody Theological Seminary and Graduate School) for his encouragement and endorsement.

Forward

Stepping back in history can be intimidating. The challenge to understand how events in distant lands and bygone days relate to everyday life in the here and now is formidable. The sheer magnitude of the centuries of time which have elapsed since our spiritual forefathers served God amid crises and difficulties, amid opposition and resistance, seemingly militates against identifying ourselves in any significant way with their life situations. Yet the Bible is not only clear but indeed forthright in declaring that those *"things (which) were written aforetime were written for our learning, that we through patience and comfort of the scriptures might have hope"* (Rom. 15:4).

If then, a study of the sagas and chronicles recorded in Scripture and an appreciation of the historical narratives are essential for our persevering in service to God, what better tool for equipping us for His work and what better method for encouraging us in our own spiritual walk than not only to study, but also to lingeringly contemplate the wondrous accounts of God's faithful servants detailed for us in the pages of the Old Testament. Across the ages man's societal context may have changed but the root problems with which he is confronted have not.

Herein lies the challenge. How do we avoid relegating to cultures of marginal relevance the very accounts designed to instruct us? How do we span the cavernous valley of centuries of history so distinct and far removed from ourselves in time and space? The answer is not found in seeking to somehow wrest the men and women of the Bible from their historical context, transplanting them in to our own times, but rather in transporting ourselves back to their days.

To this end, Dr. Estevez has provided us with a marvelously useful and immensely engaging consideration of the kings who reigned over God's people. He invites us to breathe the air and tread the streets of those who have gone before us. He draws a meticulous portrait from each biblical account and asks us to step in close and to carefully consider the greatness of God's work in the lives of men. But most importantly, Dr. Estevez leaves no doubt as to the commonality of the trials which men face no matter, the epoch of time in which they live, and of both the grace and the righteousness of God as He works out His divine plans through those who belong to Him. That love of God, which the Old Testament saints experienced in its breadth and depth, is the same love with which God still operates in our lives in the twenty-first century—for God's love never changes; it endures forever. *Dr. Jim Haesemeyer*

Dr. Roberto Estevez, a medical physician, prescribes a watchful regimen of purity for today's Christians, especially those in America and others exposed to America's sick and contagious culture.

This book is comprised of a biographical lesson from ten ancient kings of Judea. All the kings selected essentially had good spiritual health, doing *"that which was right in the eyes of God,"* but they failed in their struggle against evil, at least at one point, whether with adultery, culture, wealth, power, fame, pride, anger, anxiety, alliances, or idolatry. Eventually, the nation crumbled morally, allowing Babylon to conquer them and take Judah captive into exile.

According to the Scriptures, for a book to minister spiritually to a reader, it must influence in at least two ways—bestowing God's light and God's strength. *Our Struggle with Good and Evil* affected me, as I read it, by enhancing my discernment between good and evil in the opportunities and attractions of the day I face, and then by encouraging me to trust and obey my Saviour

Forward

in what He desires me to do. It's simple. It's powerful.

Unlike many medicines I have taken, this book tastes good, too. It is interesting and uncomplicated. Chapter by chapter, Estevez probes with a keen eye the life of each king, in its historical and biblical setting. He diagnoses spiritual strengths and ailments, and scripts each case-study in graphic and lifelike situations, so that the text reads like a novel.

Theologically, this careful Bible teacher folds the New Testament into his expositions, drawing contrasts between the times of the kings living under the Mosaic law and the Prophets, and the times of today, with its full and complete biblical revelation of God.

Practically, the author offers questions at the end of each chapter to jump-start relevant group discussions. With the chapters numbering twelve, the book can fit into the quarterly curriculum of Bible studies and Sunday-School classes.

B.W. Hopkins, Th.D.
Former Vice President, Dean, and Professor Emeritus
Moody Theological Seminary and Graduate School
Chicago, Illinois

What Could I Learn from Ancient Kings?

Many people determine success or failure in terms of social standing or the accumulation of wealth. Others judge by one's effect on society or religious influence on others.

An individual may be an outstanding success in one area while totally failing in another. The world is replete with persons who have achieved great financial prosperity yet have a disappointing home life or difficulty in interpersonal relationships.

In this book we will explore the following questions:

- By what standards does God evaluate the success of a believer's life?

- From what we read in the Bible, what criteria does He use to review ministry and service?

- What do the lives of the ancient kings of Judah—men who lived 2500 years ago—have to do with mine?

- What does it mean when the Bible says, as in 2 Chronicles 34:2, that a king *"did what was right in the sight of the LORD"*?

Turning to the study of the godly kings of Judah, we quickly recognize that, though they wore golden crowns on their heads, what was important in their lives (and what made their lives significant) was their desire to please God. Nevertheless, these kings had weaknesses and a propensity to fall...just as we do. The situations in which they found themselves were not dissimilar to our experiences. It is not by chance that the Spirit of God has recorded the lives of these men for us in the Holy Scriptures. *"For whatever things were written before were written for our learning, that we through the patience and comfort of the Scriptures might have hope"* (Rom 15:4).

God in His holiness and righteousness has not hidden the flaws of these individuals who, in their time, held the most responsible office possible. Their biographies are presented like un-retouched photographs: we see them just as they were, not as we would like to see them.

So it is that David is shown to be a champion, a man of enormous faith in God, fully convinced that God would enable him to fell the giant Goliath as if he were made of wet cardboard. We also read, however, that this same David fell into such grievous iniquity that a chain reaction of sin began that included adultery, deceit, the betrayal of a trusted servant, and murder at the hands of a third party. We see David descending the steps from the palace terrace with adultery in his heart, each step trampling the beautiful psalms of piety and justice he had penned earlier in his life. Time and again the sacred authors write, *"he did what was right, **but...** "* (2 Chron. 25:2).

The message of these kings is for us today: God still looks upon and contemplates His servants. He evaluates our work and dedication and wants us to live triumphant lives. His goal is that it could be said that each of us "did what was right," without any qualifiers. Enoch's testimony shines forth a brilliant neon sign: *"for before he was taken he had this testimony, that he pleased God"* (Heb. 11:5). We longingly hear the words of the apostle Paul as he looked back and was gratefully able to say, *"I have fought the good fight, I have finished the race, I have kept the faith"* (2 Tim. 4:7).

Some dialogues and aspects of the narratives are not found word-for-word in the Bible. I have taken some poetic license but have endeavored always to conform to the spirit and truths

Introduction

of the biblical passages. Among my goals is to illustrate well the historical context, the options before the particular monarch, and the complexities of the decision-making process.

In writing this book, I have tried to recreate the ambience and the atmosphere of these biblical narratives, to capture their significance in a deep and intimate way. To the extent that goal has been realized, I give thanks to God. I wish to exhort preachers, teachers, and indeed all believers to learn from these biblical biographies that God has given us in His Holy Word.

We are astounded at times by the gravity of the sins these kings committed. Nevertheless, in spite of all the human failures, the sovereign grace of God worked in them. In the final analysis of their lives, we read, *"And he did what was right..."* (2 Kgs. 14:3, 15:34, 22:2; 2 Chron. 25:2, 29:2, 34:2; etc.).

Part 1

A HOUSE AFTER GOD'S OWN HEART

Chapter 1

DAVID: T-SHIRT VERSUS ARMOUR

In the tranquil moments of midday, a shepherd strums his harp. A sweet melody of worship rises up to God, expressing faith in words such as,

> The LORD is my light and my salvation;
> Whom shall I fear?
> The LORD is the strength of my life;
> Of whom shall I be afraid?
>
> Psalm 27:1

The Shepherd Boy

God's Military School

Suddenly the shepherd, young David, hears a sharp, terrified bleat. A sheep is being attacked by a lion. The young man drops his instrument, grabs a long pole with a metallic point, and takes off running toward the distressed animal. As he dashes up, he sees a bloody scene. The lion is dragging away a sheep, that is still alive and bleating plaintively. The shepherd doesn't hesitate. He raises his spear and the lion releases its victim, and turns to attack David.

David's heart is beating with all its might but it is also filled with the message of the psalm, *"Whom shall I fear?"* (Ps. 27:1). With a well-placed thrust, the shepherd plunges the spear into the animal's neck. The lion falls over, mortally wounded. With gentle tenderness David approaches the sheep. He binds up the wounds with improvised materials, lifts the sheep onto his shoulders, and carries her back (Luke 15:1-6).

Many months later, in the main hall of the royal palace, King Saul meets with his military leaders. Messengers are arriving regularly with news from the battlefront. There, a giant is triumphing. Truly frightening, Goliath possesses brutal force. He is pitiless and cruel to his enemies. That much he has demonstrated many times. He is invincible. What's more, no one has volunteered to fight against Goliath, in spite of the honours and gifts the king has offered as an inducement.

The king looks around at his commanders and captains. They are experienced warriors who have been in many battles. Many of them bear the scars of wounds received in previous conflicts. In modern times these men would wear medals and battle ribbons honouring their courage and bravery.

The ruler looks at his men and asks, "Who among you has the courage to fight against Goliath?"

The men lower their eyes. None of them dares to step forward. It means sure death for the enemy is too formidable. It is a lost cause.

Enter David

"Your majesty," reports one of the servants, "the young man whom you called is here. He says he is willing to fight the giant. I think it would be useless, but he is a very resolute boy. I informed him that we are looking for a warrior, not an apprentice, but he is insistent."

"Tell him to approach," Saul replies.

The king's pavilion is spacious; ornaments adorn the walls and breathtaking rugs are lavishly spread across the floors. David enters the room with a determined step and then

David: T-shirt Versus Armour

respectfully greets the sovereign and all present. He is good-looking and muscular, between the ages of sixteen and eighteen, but his shepherd's attire is simple. The military leaders cannot hide their mocking smiles as they think to themselves, "And this one? Who does he think he is?"

The shepherd boy says firmly and calmly, *"Let no man's heart fail because of him; your servant will go and fight with this Philistine"* (1 Sam. 17:32).

Saul responds, *"You are not able to go against this Philistine to fight with him; for you are a youth, and he is a man of war from his youth"* (1 Sam. 17:33)

With humility and in submission to the king, David explains, *"Your servant used to keep his father's sheep, and when a lion or a bear came and took a lamb out of the flock, I went out after it and struck it, and delivered the lamb from its mouth; and when it arose against me, I caught it by its beard, and struck and killed it"* (1 Sam. 17:34-35)

The generals glance at one another as if to say, Yet another of those amazing exploits that are impossible to prove.

David continues, *"Your servant has killed both a lion and a bear; and this uncircumcised Philistine will be like one of them, seeing he has defied the armies of the living God…The LORD, who delivered me from the paw of the lion and from the paw of the bear, He will deliver me from the hand of this Philistine"* (1 Sam. 17:36-37).

The king was impressed by the young man's fortitude. Because neither he nor his battle-hardened warriors have stepped forward to fight the giant, Saul offers his own armor. So he clothes David with his armor, puts a bronze helmet on his head, and adds a coat of mail. (What Saul didn't know, however, was that symbolically he is relinquishing his royal position. By his own actions, he is investing the young shepherd with royal authority.)

Saul had a great deal of confidence in that armor. Without a doubt, it was of the highest quality and had cost much to create. Surely the armor was the best that gold could buy. Nevertheless, of what benefit was it when pitted against such a strong enemy? The king did not dare to put it on nor to venture out against him.

The young shepherd fastens the sword to his armor and tries to walk, but he cannot. David must have looked like a robot or a science-fiction character. *"I cannot walk with these, for I have not tested them"* (1 Sam. 17:39).

David quickly removes the heavy gear. That armor, though well suited for defense, would have guaranteed a complete defeat. The only chance of victory lay in attack, not in defense. The proud king's helmet would not protect the shepherd's head. The coat of mail belonging to the man whom God had rejected would not protect David's heart. The sword of the man disqualified by God because of disobedience would never enjoy God's blessing. The simple shirt of the young man of faith would afford far better protection than the strongest breastplate of the king whose disobedience had left him cast aside by God.

The breastplate, the helmet, and the sword were left in to a corner of the palace hall. The generals were still laughing at the comical appearance of the young man sagging under the weight of the ill-fitting armor. Yet with a respectful salute to the king and the others, David leaves the palace to undertake his venture.

The news travels quickly and soon reaches both camps. Goliath has an opponent who will defend the banner of Israel.

David and the Giant (1 Samuel 17)

In the dwelling of the king who had been disobedient to God, the atmosphere is heavy and wearying. David has left the royal palace and once outside he feels free, as if a weighty oppression has melted away.

The Battle Begins

The Israelites are once again retreating desperately. *"When all the men of Israel saw the man, they fled from him and were greatly afraid"* (1 Sam. 17:24). The Israelite soldiers run aimlessly, chaotically. The giant has come out to provoke the God of Israel. But there is a rumour that someone is willing to defend Israel. "Who could it be?" the Jews ask one another. "Some famous general? Some battle-hardened commander?"

David: T-shirt Versus Armour

When the soldiers learn that the one who is willing to challenge the giant, the one who is to be the defender of Israel, is nothing more than a young shepherd boy with no military experience whatsoever, they are scornful.

"He's totally crazy!" some say.

"The poor guy. He won't last a minute. He must be some sort of fanatic," say others.

Still others decide that the young man must be insolent or someone merely seeking to make a name for himself. But the reality is that David is simply an individual who has a profound faith in the Lord of Hosts.

The army of Israel gathers to watch the encounter from a hillside a prudent distance from the enemy forces. The young shepherd walks toward the stream which meanders through the Valley of Elah. We don't know what went through the mind of David as he walks toward the giant. Perhaps David considers the possibility that Goliath has brothers or friends who are giants as well (1 Chron. 20:5; 2 Sam. 21:22). In the streambed there are many water-worn rocks and David chooses five. They are smooth and will make good projectiles. For centuries these stones have been honed by the constant polishing action of the water and the buffing of stone upon stone. Those rocks which for ages have been ground down will now have the chance to deliver a blow themselves!

David approaches the field where Goliath habitually marches as he taunts the terrified Israelites and shouts blasphemies against the God of Israel. The Israeli soldiers stand transfixed, waiting to see what will happen. The young man approaches Goliath with complete assurance. *"The eyes of the LORD are toward the righteous, and His ears are open to their cry"* (Ps. 34:15).

It is not that David has no fear. Surely at this moment his feelings are complex and difficult to explain. His heart is thudding in his chest because he realizes that he bears a great responsibility. He is not unaware that he is defending the honour of Israel. He knows well that if he commits but the slightest error, the giant will destroy him. It is for this very reason he feels the strong conviction that the Lord is at his side and that God will give him the victory. Certainly David knows that, humanly speaking, there is no hope of defeating the giant. David's "resume" and his "curriculum vitae" are not very impressive. He has, however, been in the Musical Conservatory of the Lord and he has attended the Military School of God. There, in his struggles with the savage lion and the ferocious bear, he has learned that God can give strength and victory. He knows that he is able, by God's help, to overcome his paralyzing fears. The Lord has shown His faithfulness many times in the past. David is absolutely certain that He will do so in the same way at this moment.

When David charges toward the colossus, it is as if he is looking beyond to something even bigger beyond the giant. Psalm 16 may reveal his feelings, *"I have set the Lord always before me; because He is at my right hand I shall not be moved"* (1 Sam. 17:8).

Goliath's armor-bearer carries a shield capable of withstanding nearly very kind of projectile. But the giant did not realize that David has an armor-bearer both invisible and invincible.

Nobody has ever beaten Goliath. Usually his enemies have fled in terror when they merely saw him approaching. *"When the Philistine looked and saw David, he disdained him, for he was but a youth and ruddy, with a handsome appearance…And the Philistine cursed him by his gods"* (1 Sam. 17:42-43). With these words, Goliath seals his own death sentence. The Israelite soldiers were looking on with fear. Most of them have no doubts how it would end. "The poor guy," say some, "He's so young to die." Some of the Jews are praying to the Lord for a miracle. They know that Jehovah, who had brought them out of Egypt by his strong arm, could deliver once again.

The voices of the Philistines, in contrast, gather strength as they cheer Goliath on. "Long live Goliath!" "Yea, Goliath!"

The drums and the cymbals of the Philistines fill the air with infernal sounds, presaging Goliath's triumph. The rhythm grows in strength and more intensity.

David: T-shirt Versus Armour

When a Giant Shrinks

Then Goliath signals and the music abruptly stops. With a commanding voice he shouts, *"Come to me, and I will give your flesh to the birds of the sky and the beasts of the field!"* (1 Sam. 17:44).

Enormous applause erupts from the Philistine camp. Again the cheers are heard, "Long live Goliath!"

The attention shifts to the young shepherd. He has no armor, no shield, no sword. He bears only a sling and an unfailing trust in the faithfulness of God. David's voice resonates through the valley. His words are clear and strong. There is not a tinge of fear or dread. *"You come to me with a sword , with a spear, and with a javelin. But I come to you in the name of the LORD of hosts, the God of the armies of Israel, whom you have defied"* (1 Sam. 17:45). David pauses briefly. If we could have seen the face of the giant, partially hidden behind his helmet, we would have found a mocking, cruel smile.

The young shepherd continues, *"This day the LORD will deliver you up into my hand, and I will strike you and take your head from you…that all the earth may know that there is a God in Israel …this assembly shall know that the LORD does not save with sword and spear; for the battle is the LORD's and He will give you into our hands"* (1 Sam. 17:46-47).

"Enough," the giant says to himself, "I am going to teach him who I am!" The Philistine rises and strides toward David.

Any one of us in a similar situation would have been deathly frightened and run or at least stood frozen, preparing ourselves to withstand the onslaught, but David, *"ran toward the army to meet the Philistine"* (1 Sam. 17:48).

The crowds of soldiers cannot believe what they see. David, instead of fleeing for his life, is actually running toward his enemy. "The poor little guy," many are thinking, "He'll be ground to bits."

But then David thrusts his hand into his bag and takes out a stone. He slings the stone and then releases it. The stone strikes the Philistine on his forehead. The stone sinks into his forehead and the giant falls face down (1 Sam. 17:49).

Let us watch in slow motion the trajectory of David's project-ile. The rock is hurled with tremendous force and seems to know precisely where to go. It travels with the precision of a radar-guided missile, burying itself in the forehead of the enemy.

David's actions are like those of theatrical players who have practiced their scenes so many times that they can act their parts in a completely natural way. David does not pause in his rush toward Goliath. Everything takes place in a matter of seconds. Before the armor-bearer can react, David grasps the giant's enormous sword in his hand. The armor-bearer runs away in terror.

"Therefore David ran and stood over the Philistine, took his sword and drew it out of its sheath and killed him, and cut off his head with it" (1 Sam. 17:51).

"No, No! It can't be!" shout the throngs of Philistines.

"Yes! Yes! Praise the LORD" shout the jubilant Hebrews.

Thus David killed the Philistine giant with a sling and a stone; he killed him without having a sword in his hand.

David returns to King Saul with a grotesque trophy, the head of Goliath, in his hand. The multitudes, who were scarcely able to believe what they had seen, rush to see if it could indeed be true. Their enemy, the invincible, has been defeated. There is no longer any doubt. In the hand of David is the definitive evidence that the triumph is complete. The Hebrews hasten after the fleeing Philistines and achieve an overwhelming victory.

The Bible Back-Story

How Could It Happen?

This account reminds us of the time when the Philistines captured the Ark of the Covenant and placed it in their pagan temple. *"And when the people of Ashdon arose early in the morning, there was Dagon, fallen on its face to the earth before the Ark of the LORD. So they took Dagon and set it in its place again. And when*

David: T-shirt Versus Armour

they arose early the next morning, there was Dagon, fallen on its face to the ground before the ark of the LORD" (1 Sam. 5:3-4a).

Some scholars have postulated that when Goliath insulted the God of Israel, he moved his hand up and that this action resulted in his helmet being raised and exposing his forehead. The biblical text does not say that the stone penetrated the helmet but it does say that it buried itself in Goliath's forehead.

David probably used his shepherd's sling while still running toward the giant and may have released the stone from a distance of twenty to thirty yards. Normally a person standing erect, when receiving a frontal impact, would fall backwards. But the Bible specifically states that Goliath fell forward. Perhaps this is symbolic of a spiritual blow to Goliath's pride.

There is no need to assume that the stone possessed supernatural power or had attained extraordinary velocity. The miracle was that David executed the plan God had shown him and all subsequent events occurred precisely as "programmed." God had determined the blaspheming giant would die and that is exactly what happened. This was all accomplished by a young man who had consecrated himself to God to serve Him and to trust in Him.

Medical Notes

Some medical doctors have tried to explain Goliath's enormous stature by postulating a benign tumor of the pituitary gland. This gland secretes human growth hormone and if a tumor appeared during childhood development, it could result in gigantism. According to this explanation, the stone's impact on a person with this type of tumor would provoke the falling down as described in the biblical account. However, this theory fails to explain why Goliath had a brother who was a giant as well. It is true that there is a rare form of genetic disease called MEN1 syndrome (Multiple Endocrine Adenoma). These types of tumors are often accompanied by a loss of lateral vision due to the compression of the optic nerve by the tumor (*hemianopsia*).

Athletes of any age can be killed by the impact of a baseball that has been thrown with great speed. These "dry blows" can cause death in certain susceptible people. This can occur even with requisite chest protection. From the medical point of view, it is improbable that the stone would have caused immediate death. The Jewish historian Josephus states that the stone penetrated the skull and lodged in the brain.[1]

The Struggles in Our Lives

By Whose Power?

How was David able to overcome a lion and even a bear? Did he achieve remarkable feats by his own strength and ability or was it by some supernatural power which he had received from the Lord?

Some commentators attempt to avoid the problem by surmising that the lion was of a smaller variety than common lions and that the bear was not as ferocious. If this were so, the achievements would scarcely be worth mentioning to Saul. On the contrary, the two wild beasts were frightening; the only manner by which David was able to defeat them was by the specific intervention of God, not by the strength of Tarzan. David clearly said, *"The LORD, who delivered me from the paw of the lion and from the paw of the bear"* (1 Sam. 17:37).

In the same way, we cannot defeat Satan by our own strength, but with the help of God we can be victorious. As the apostle Paul wrote, *"the God of peace will crush Satan under your feet shortly"* (Rom 16:20). I might be able to defend myself from a lion if I had a good knife; my bigger problem would be a paralyzing fear.

Every detail of the biblical text clearly shows us that this enemy was very dangerous. He would have been about nine feet in stature and would have weighing around six hundred to eight hundred pounds. His helmet and the rest of his armor would have weighed some 130 pounds; his spear point, about 15 pounds. He was a warrior who was invincible.[2]

The king tried to dissuade David citing his youth and lack of experience. At times those who sincerely want to help us

David: T-shirt Versus Armour

unwittingly discourage us. The life of David is an example of one who is time and again under appreciated. His superiors see him as someone less than the ideal man for the job or they consider him as lacking in one quality or the other. How easy it would be for us to become discouraged under similar circumstances! The world is full of individuals who tell us, "You can't do it."

Paul had an answer for those who habitually declare, "You can't." He rejoiced in the words, *"I can do all things through Christ who strengthens me"* (Phil 4:13). David was young and clearly had not received formal military instruction. But he had been trained by God. The Lord had prepared him. The encounter he had with the lion and with the bear were not casual accidents. God had orchestrated those events and they had a purpose. Surely the first time he was confronted by a dangerous wild animal he had felt the terror that such a situation naturally produces. Perhaps the shepherd attacked the wild beast having a shovel with a sharp blade tip. How easy it would have been for David to have simply abandoned the sheep. No doubt it had already been wounded and would be likely to die anyway (Amos 3:12).

But David didn't have that mindset. He felt personally responsible for each sheep. In a similar way, the Lord Jesus cares for the sheep that the Father has entrusted to Him (John 17:12). What a beautiful image of the security of eternal salvation! If we but let the Lord teach us, we'll be well equipped for the spiritual struggle.

Symbolically King Saul had deposed himself when he gave his armor to David. We run the same risk within the local church by not fulfilling and developing the spiritual gifts we have received from the Lord. God will raise up another who will perhaps be less gifted or equipped for the service to which we were called. *"Therefore take the talent from him, and give it to him who has ten talents"* (Matt. 25:28).

What would have been considered logical by human standards, the use of the king's armor, would actually have assured a disaster. May the Lord help us understand that *"the weapons of our warfare are not carnal"* (2 Cor. 10:4). Our battle is of the Lord and we must use the means and methods that He permits. In spiritual things, the end never justifies the means.

David's only chance of winning against Goliath was to attack rather than to defend himself. What possible defense is there against a lance point weighing fifteen pounds? Remember, when everything seems lost, the Lord can still lead us to triumph. *"Who is he who overcomes the world, but he who believes that Jesus is the Son of God?"* (1 John 5:5).

Facing Our Goliaths

We all have moments when we must confront an enemy who appears invincible. Nevertheless, when everything seems lost, as believers we can attain victory by trusting in our God.

David's battle was not a spontaneous act of heroism or foolhardiness. Although not explicit in the biblical account, surely David spent time in fervent prayer seeking the Lord and His will. He received an unambiguous answer from God. God instructed David precisely what to do, namely, to use his natural skills such as wielding a sling. Still, it was not David's talent or his aim that counted most but God's perfect plan, which was to be fulfilled in every detail.

David picked up five stones—one for Goliath and extras in case Goliath's brother (1 Chron. 20:5) or friends joined in the fray. Then David ran toward the giant, resolved to do what he had to do. Many times, we are more like the sons of Ephraim, who *"being armed and carrying bows, Turned back in the day of battle"* (Ps. 78:9). Well equipped and with an illustrious history of bravery and courage, yet they retreated and fled instead of standing firm in battle.

Goliath threatened to give the body of David to the birds of the air and wild beasts of the field, an image repugnant and terrifying. Obviously, he intended to thoroughly demoralize his opponent. Now as in David's time, God has words for us that surpass the worst threats: *"And do not fear those who kill the body but cannot kill the soul. But rather fear Him who is able to destroy both soul and body in hell"* (Matt. 10:28).

David: T-shirt Versus Armour

David's sling shot found its mark, but the young shepherd also did not give the giant an opportunity to rise again. Cutting off his head was the only manner in which he could be sure that the enemy was totally annihilated. Although this sounds crude and brutal, the truth is that life can often be that way. The enemy simply must be killed and destroyed. The spiritual temptations in our lives must never be pampered or even tolerated; rather, they must be totally eliminated. For the moment we live in this present world system and cannot destroy, but we can "die" to it (Gal 5:16-6:15).

Goliath went into the fight with a sword, a spear, and other armaments. David went forth with a Name, the Name of God. The battle was much more than a physical confrontation; it was a spiritual contest. In the words of Paul, *"we do not wrestle against flesh and blood"* (Eph. 6:12). David said,

> For by You I can run against a troop,
> By my God I can leap over a wall.
>
> Psalm 18:29

We have the protection of the Lord as well. *"The angel of the LORD encamps all around those who fear Him, And delivers them"* (Ps 34:7).

Using Our Gifts

A Christian needs the instruction of God, a teaching that cannot be imparted from human beings. This training proceeds from a personal study of God's Word, accompanied by the exercise of prayer. David began such preparation in his youth while still caring for sheep. There he learned to trust the Almighty with total confidence.

Because of his gift of music, David was brought to the royal palace. Each of us has a gift like the harp of David. If we will let ourselves be used by God, we will be able to do the work that our hearts desire. The training of David in the house of Saul was truly his university experience. Solid leadership that is going to be effective over the long run requires adequate preparation. While it is true that many great people of God have never attended a university or a seminary, nevertheless these places can be of great blessing when they are used appropriately. In the long term, short cuts can prove to be paths that are very tedious and slow. David could have asked himself if he were wasting his time by providing therapeutic music when he had many other abilities that he wanted to use, but he had to wait until God's time.

Saul, on the other hand, was chosen to be king of Israel, but by the time of the confrontation with the giant he had lost the ability to lead. Conspicuous by its absence was his willingness to be in the place of responsibility and danger. From the moment he determined to fight the one who challenged all of Israel, however, David became a leader, the role God had for him.

David looked at Goliath through the glasses of faith and the giant became a dwarf. We too can declare, *"If God is for us, who can be against us?"* (Rom 8:31b).

Comparison And Contrast For Expansion

Contrasts between Goliath and the Lord Jesus

Goliath	Jesus
Tall and domineering	Of a humble spirit (John 13)
His presence inspires terror	*"My peace I leave with you."*
Appeared to be invincible but actually lost	Appeared to have been conquered on the cross but actually was victorious
Mocks and blasphemes God	Is honoured by God
Came to kill	Came to give life
His defeat was final	His victory was complete

David: T-shirt Versus Armour

David, a man who was little esteemed

- By his father: *"There is still the youngest"* (1 Sam. 16:16).
- By the bear and the lion which attacked him: *"When it arose against me, I...caught it and killed it"* (1 Sam. 17:35).
- By Goliath: He *"disdained him for he was only a youth"* (1 Sam. 17:42).
- By his wife Michal: *"she despised him in her heart"* (2 Sam. 6:16).
- By King Abimilech: *"Have I need of madmen that you have brought me this fellow?"* (1 Sam. 21:15).
- By himself: *"Whom do you pursue? A dead dog? A flea?"* (1 Sam. 24:14).

The Sword

- The sword made useless because of disobedience: The sword of Saul (1 Sam. 17:39)
- The unique sword, *"there is none like it"*: The sword of Goliath (1 Sam. 21:9)
- The sword which imparts courage: *"the sword of the Lord and the sword of Gideon"* (Judg. 7:20)
- The sword of forwardness: *"Jesus said to Peter, 'Put your sword into its sheath'"* (John 18:11)
- The sword which pierces: *"Because the sword is living and powerful"* (Heb. 4:12)
- The sword of the glorified Lord: *"Out of His mouth went a sharp, two-edged sword"* (Rev. 1:16)

Discussion Starters

1. What short phrases would describe the following swords from the Old Testament?

   The sword of Saul (1 Sam. 17:39)

   The sword of Goliath (1 Sam. 21:9)

The swords of the Lord and of Gideon (Judg. 7:20)

2. Do the same with these swords from the New Testament:

   The sword of Peter (John 18:11)

   The sword that is the Word (Heb. 4:12)

   The sword of the glorified Lord (Rev. 1:16)

3. None of us will have to fight an actual Philistine giant, but we all face giant struggles with good and evil. Consider the following enemies of the human soul, particularly of youth. What are the tactics of the "Goliath"...

   ...of alcohol and drugs?

   ...of sexual sins?

   ...of other sins of the flesh?

   ...of this present world?

   ...who is Satan?

4. What is the most persistent "Goliath" in your life? What weapon from David's story might help you in your struggle?

Chapter 2

DAVID: FROM THE ROOFTOP TO THE BASEMENT

"Goodbye, my love," says the warrior as he pauses by the door. "I love you with all my soul."

The beautiful young wife replies, "My beloved husband, I love *you* with all my heart. My first prayer in the morning will be to ask the Lord to protect you on the battlefield and to bless you. My last request in the evening will be that the Lord be with you. I beg you to take care of yourself and hurry back to me. I will be waiting for you with my arms open."

The Household of Uriah

The Girl Next Door

Her eyes brim with tears. She has had to say goodbye to her husband several times in the past, but this particular time grave misgivings well up in her heart.

Uriah, a brave and distinguished soldier, attempts to hide his emotions. He hugs Bathsheba, kisses her on the forehead, and says, "May the peace of the Lord be with you." He turns and walks away quickly, so as not to make the farewell any more painful than it already is. The wife watches her husband leave until he disappears from her sight along the twisting streets of Jerusalem.

The two have known each other since childhood. He was a little older, but the difference was not great. He loved her even then. Their wedding was in accordance with Jewish customs. Not only during the wedding ceremony but in the days of feasting that followed, everyone was full of joy and happy for the young couple. She was a beautiful woman, warm-hearted, godly, and loving. He was one of the King's "valiant men," renowned for his courage and virtue. At home, Uriah was the perfect husband. He sought to treat Bathsheba with absolute affection and tenderness. He loved and respected her.

Several weeks have passed since Uriah departed for battle. His loyal wife often looks longingly out the window of their house and wonders if a messenger might bring news of her husband's well-being. Sadly, little news is forthcoming.

Just a Glance

A short distance from Uriah's home is the royal palace. In spite of the fact that it was the time of year when "*kings go out to battle*" (2 Sam. 11:1), King David has decided to remain in Jerusalem. On this particular afternoon, the king is not feeling well. He decides to take a short nap, but it isn't until the sun is nearly set that David finally arises. With little else to do, he climbs the steps to the terraced roof of the palace. Bored, he looks up at the darkening sky with its orange-red tones. Then he gazes at the horizon, across the city, and to the mountains.

Finally, David glances down at the houses beneath his palace. There he sees a young woman, beautiful and demure, who, believing that no one can see her, is bathing. Instead of turning away, David fixes his gaze and his thoughts on her. From this very moment, the life of David begins a slow but inexorable decline.

The King descends from the terrace and calls his servants. He inquires as to the identity of the woman who lives in that house. He carefully omits mentioning, of course, the circumstances in which he had seen her. The servants hide a smile. Everyone knows that Bathsheba is stunningly beautiful—a "Miss Israel."

"Your Majesty," replies one of the servants, *"Is this not Bathsheba, the daughter of Eliam, the wife of Uriah the Hittite?"* (2 Sam. 11:3).

Conflicting thoughts wage war in King David's mind. He well knows that the Law of God specifically condemns adultery (Ex 20:14), but his passions have taken over.

Invitation to Temptation

He turns to his servant and gives an order that he himself can scarcely believe he is giving. "Go and bring her."

David's messengers step into the large hall and address Bathsheba. "My lady, we have a communication for you from the King. We are not at liberty to declare it before others because we are on a 'state mission.'"

The wife of Uriah gestures and her servants retire. Thinking the messengers bring word of her husband, she asks eagerly, "What is the message?"

One of the men replies, "His Majesty, the King, has invited you to dine with him. His Highness feels very lonely and it is well known how much he enjoys conversation…"

"When?"

"Today. That is, right now."

"How many others have been invited?" asks Bathsheba.

The messenger hesitates for a moment and then says, "You are the only one."

Bathsheba is not naïve. A cold shiver jolts her body. "I will, of course, accept the invitation."

She retires to her bedroom and confides in her maidservant, a woman who has been with her since childhood. The maidservant grows pale. "My lady, please do not go! The King should not force you to go without your husband being present. I'm fearful that he has intentions."

Bathsheba is confused. She has the opportunity of a lifetime. And what can be wrong with merely going to dine at the palace if one has been invited?

As she leaves her house, none of the promises of love she made to Uriah come to mind. On one side of the threshold, she had been a faithful spouse; on the other, she becomes a woman who betrays her adoring husband.

When Bathsheba returns home in the morning, the servants greet her, albeit with long faces. The house seems gloomy and dark, even though the windows are wide open. Later, as she sits at the table for a meal, she looks at Uriah's empty chair and imagines their tender conversations. Bathsheba turns her head as if to avoid his gaze.

Messages Sent and Received

Best Laid Plans

It seems like a routine day for King David. One of his attendants announces himself and declares, "Majesty, I have been given a message for you." King David receives the scroll with interest, perhaps even with a little eagerness. The communication may prove to be something to relieve the monotony of the day. The monarch removes the seal from the scroll, reads the message, and immediately grows pale.

The text is brief: *"I am with child"* (2 Sam. 11:5). In a rage he flings the note into the fire smoldering in the brazier. He begins to pace from one side of the spacious chamber to the other. Suddenly a smile appears on his lips. He has a plan that cannot fail. He quickly scrawls out a note to Joab, his general, in which he orders that officer Uriah be sent to him immediately.

Days later and hundreds of miles away, Joab reads the message from the king. He is perplexed. Uriah is an important officer, but he has never been a counselor to the monarch. And why the urgency?

David: From the Rooftop to the Basement

A few days pass until a weary Uriah arrives in Jerusalem. In spite of the long, tiring journey, the faithful officer proceeds directly to the palace. Immediately he is introduced to the grand chamber and presented to the king.

"Your Majesty," says Uriah, "General Joab sends his respects and his wishes for the peace of the Lord to be with you."

King David responds, "I'm pleased to see that you are well. I would very much like to know how things are going on the battlefront. In particular, how is the morale of the troops?"

The officer informs the king of all the affairs about which he inquires. After a while, David changes his tone and speaks very solemnly. All those present are listening. "Officer Uriah, I want you to know how grateful I and the people of Israel are for your service to the nation. There may be a promotion of rank for your invaluable and extraordinary dedication to duty."

Uriah replies, "I am undeserving of such an honour. I certainly was not expecting anything."

After a few more pleasantries, the king courteously dismisses Uriah with a gesture.

The Honourable Officer

From the palace, Uriah can see his home—the dim light of the lamps are barely visible in the windows. For a moment he considers going home even if only to pass by, but he is restrained, as if an invisible hand were holding him back. He is surprised to see several palace servants walking up to the door of his house. The king's servants have brought trays replete with gifts and delicacies.

The following morning the king rises with a feeling of optimism. The threat of being accused of adultery has vanished for he quite naturally assumes Uriah passed the night with his wife. When the child is born, the adoring father will never suspect anything. Soon, however, David learns from his servants that Uriah did not sleep in his own house last night. "We tried to encourage him to go home to rest in his own house, but he wouldn't listen to us. In fact, he refused to do so."

After much pacing and deliberation, the king orders Uriah to appear before him. He says forcefully, "You just returned to Jerusalem from a long journey. Why haven't you gone to your house? Why haven't you greeted your wife?"

Uriah answers, *"The ark and Israel and Judah are dwelling in tents, and my lord Joab and the servants of my lord are encamped in the open fields. Shall I then go to my house to eat and drink, and to lie with my wife? As you live, and as your soul lives, I will not do this thing"* (2 Sam. 11:11).

"I acknowledge your keen sense of responsibility to duty," says David, recovering. "I'm pleased to have officers with such dedication as yours. I will expect you to dine with me this evening."

As the evening goes on, King David urges Uriah to have another cup of wine, but the officer says that he is not accustomed to so much drink and is already feeling dizzy. The king insists that they toast General Joab, hoping that Uriah will be drunk enough to put aside his allegiance to duty and return to his own home that night.

But Uriah does not return home. His sense of responsibility is greater than the effects of the alcohol. Even in his state of drunkenness he remains faithful to his moral obligations.

The following day David sends Uriah back to the battlefront. Uriah is honoured to have been entrusted with a letter to Joab, written by the king's own hand. Uriah has no idea that the same hand that had written so many glorious psalms had just written a letter ordering his murder.

The Death of Uriah

Joab opens the letter from King David. Unbelievably, it reads, *"Set Uriah in the forefront of the hottest battle, and retreat from him, that he may be struck down and die"* (2 Sam 11:15). General Joab wonders how Uriah could have so offended the king to deserve such drastic measures. But he knows he must carry out the order.

Early the next day, Uriah and his squadron set out for the west wall, hoping to breech it. The brave officer leads his men in the attack but soon is hit by one arrow, and then another. Uriah the Hittite is dead.

Following the brief battle, Joab dispatches a messenger to the king. The messenger relates the details of the failed strategy to take the city. The monarch is angry. The messenger continues, *"The archers shot from the wall at your servants; and some of the king's servants are dead, and your servant Uriah the Hittite is dead also"* (2 Sam. 11:24).

Immediately David's temper abates. He represses a faint smile and says calmly, *"Thus you shall say to Joab: 'Do not let this thing displease you, for the sword devours one as well as another. Strengthen your attack against the city, and overthrow it.' So encourage him"* (2 Sam. 11:25).

The news of Uriah's death travels quickly through the royal palace. Uriah's widow, Bathsheba, mourns for her husband as is the custom. When the period of mourning is ended, King David sends for her to live with him at the palace. The servants begin making calculations because Bathsheba seems well along in her pregnancy. And the most interesting aspect is it has been more than a year since Uriah had been with his wife!

"She became his wife and bore him a son. But the thing that David had done displeased the LORD" (2 Sam. 11:27).

The months pass and palace life has returned to its normal routine. But there is one notable difference the servants have observed—the king himself has changed. In the mornings the king no longer sings the beautiful hymns he had composed. There were a few times when he attempts to sing, but it was as if his voice has become hoarse and calloused. A knot seems to form in his throat (Ps. 51:15). At other times David sits down to strum his harp but it is as though it were out of tune. After a few attempts he sets it aside, sometimes for weeks.

David no longer smiles. Those attending him during the night say he is finding it hard to sleep. He often paces back and forth in his bedchamber and is heard talking to himself. The servants and attendants cannot understand the meaning of what he is saying. He often repeats a single, short, phrase, *"Do not cast me away from Your presence, And do not take Your Holy Spirit from me"* (Ps. 51:11).

There are occasional days that things seem to go well, but soon the mood changes for the worse again. King David seems to have lost his appetite and he is losing weight. In the morning he complains of how his body is suffering and of the restless nights that have now become the norm; his bones seem to ache continually (Ps. 38). The servants say his prayers are short and that there are days when he does not pray at all. He has no peace or joy. The palace staff says that he acts as though he sees something, something that is deeply troubling to him, and he is desperately trying to close his eyes to it.

A Prophet Speaks

The Tale Is Told

One day a servant announces to the king the prophet Nathan has come to speak with him. The king orders the prophet to be shown into the great hall, where King David will receive him. Nathan is an old man, but his manner invites respect. With dignity he steps slowly into the hall.

"Good day, Prophet Nathan," greets King David. "To what do I owe the pleasure of your visit?"

With a look of discernment, Nathan says, "I would like to ask my king to advise me concerning a difficult and complex situation that has arisen. It is a legal matter."

"Explain it to me!" says the king, his curiosity aroused.

"There were two men in a city, one was rich and the other poor," begins Nathan. The king shrugs his shoulders as if saying, "Such is life."

The prophet continues, "The rich man had many sheep and much cattle, but the poor man had nothing more than a small lamb."

"Yes, I know there are inequalities in life," interrupts the king, "but, what can be done?"

David: From the Rooftop to the Basement

Nathan speaks again, "But the poor man had nothing except the small lamb which he had bought and raised. The lamb had come to be part of the family. It was cherished by his children."

The king is puzzled by the lengthy manner in which the prophet is presenting his story and wants him to get to the point. He impatiently says, "Yes, I know there are those who love God's creatures and treat them well. Some people have good hearts."

The old prophet gives the king a pointed glance and continues, "The lamb ate their bread and drank from their cup."

For a moment, King David reflects on the days of his youth, "When I was a shepherd, many times I fed my father's sheep." David grows silent and once more Nathan continues, "The lamb slept with the family. He had almost become one of the family."

"Well," David says, "perhaps you are exaggerating things a bit. Animals are animals and people are people."

Nathan repeats the words, slowly, "The family had bought the lamb. They had raised him. The children played with the lamb and the lamb ate of their food and drank from their cup. They treated the lamb almost like a child."

David grows impatient at what he views as unnecessary emphasis and excessive detail. Impatiently he once more interrupts, "Nathan, I've truly enjoyed your story, but regretfully I have a rather busy day. A king's obligations are sometimes overwhelming."

"I beg my king's indulgence and I will finish the story now," replies the prophet. "A visitor arrived at the rich man's house. The rich man, not wanting to take of his own sheep or cattle to provide for the visitor, took the lamb from the poor man, killed it and gave it for food to his guest."

"Why did the poor man not resist?" responds King David, his emotions suddenly aroused.

"Yes, he tried to, but the rich man came with many servants and they seized the lamb by force. You can imagine how the poor man wept as the men tied up the lamb to carry him away and kill it. The poor man pleaded with the men, 'Please,

I bought the lamb; I raised it; I fed it.' But the entreaties of the poor man were in vain."

"Did the rich man provide any explanation for his actions?"

"Yes," he said, 'I am the one who gives the orders around here and I do as I please.'"

By now King David is on his feet. His face is red with anger. His eyes are blazing with fury. He raises his arm and declares, *"As the Lord lives, the man who has done this shall surely die!"* (2 Sam. 12:5).

Then King David extends his arm forward in a gesture of authority, "The rich man shall pay four times the cost of the lamb because he committed such an unmerciful act and because he showed no compassion."

There is a period of profound silence. The king sits down on his throne once again, his face still livid with emotion. The servants see the king's indignation and they themselves are deeply moved by the prophet's account. They stand rigidly at attention expectantly awaiting the king's instructions to execute his ruling. With a commanding voice King David declares, "I decree that the man will pay for the lamb four times over!"

Crime and Punishment

For a moment Nathan stands before the king in silence. Then he raises his hand and points his finger directly at King David. *"You are the man!"* (2 Sam. 12:7) he shouts.

Instantly King David's face turns white as chalk. One by one the accusations fall upon him like salvos of cannon fire.

> Thus says the Lord God of Israel: "I anointed you king over Israel, and I delivered you from the hand of Saul. I gave you your master's house and your master's wives into your keeping, and gave you the house of Israel and Judah. And if that had been too little, I also would have given you much more! Why have you despised the commandment of the Lord, to do evil in His sight? You have killed Uriah the

Hittite with the sword; you have taken his wife to be your wife, and have killed him with the sword of the people of Ammon. Now therefore, the sword shall never depart from your house, because you have despised Me, and have taken the wife of Uriah the Hittite to be your wife." Thus says the Lord: "Behold, I will raise up adversity against you from your own house; and I will take your wives before your eyes and give them to your neighbor, and he shall lie with your wives in the sight of this sun. For you did it secretly, but I will do this thing before all Israel, before the sun."

2 Samuel 12:7-12

All is deathly silent. Then the king rises from the throne, steps down from the platform, and falls on his knees. He raises his arms and sobs, *"I have sinned against the LORD"* (2 Sam. 12:13).

After a time, Nathan, with a lowered voice, responds, "The LORD has also taken away your sin; you shall not die. However because by this deed you have given occasion to the enemies of the LORD to blaspheme, the child also that is born to you shall surely die" (2 Sam. 12:13-14).

The Bible Back-Story

Family History

Bathsheba was the daughter of Eliam, also called Ammiel, who was the son of Ahithophel (2 Sam. 23:34; 1 Chron. 3:5). During the rebellion of Absalom, Ahithophel provided valuable counsel to him to use against David—undoubtedly to avenge the shame committed against his granddaughter.

As was common practice, while in Hebron David had six wives and each bore a son (2 Sam. 3:2-5). Later, in Jerusalem, David had four children with Bathsheba, plus nine more sons and a daughter, Tamar. He also had children with his concubines, though their names are not specified (1 Chron. 3:1-9).

The Hittite

Uriah the Hittite was one of the valiant men of David, perhaps one of the officers of the special regiment (2 Sam. 23:39). His reluctance to return to his wife while in Jerusalem may have been dictated by a policy of sexual abstention during military campaigns (1 Sam. 21:4-5).

The Hittites themselves were a people group dwelling to the north of Israel. They had achieved a highly developed culture. It is probable that some of the descendants of the Hittites had emigrated from their lands about a century previous to this account and had settled in the land of Palestine following the collapse of the Hittite empire.[1]

In 2 Samuel 11 we read that Uriah was killed by arrows but in the next chapter that he was killed by the sword. Likely he was felled by arrows and later killed with a sword. Additionally, the word *sword* can include all types of weapons. Although his high rank would have permitted Joab to defy the order of the king, he nevertheless obeyed. This gave him leverage; he was now able to "blackmail" the monarch. Uriah dies as a hero. In contrast, the day would come when Joab would die as a coward, clinging to the horns of the altar (1 Kgs. 2:28).

Guilt and Remorse

Nathan's accusation — *"You are the man!"* (2 Sam. 12:7) — may well be the most dramatic sentence in the entire Old Testament. The words strike deep into the heart of the man in whom God's mercy was at work.

We must not conclude, however, that until the time of Nathan's visit the king lived as if nothing had happened. In Psalm 51, written immediately after the accusing visit by the prophet, we see clearly David's suffering and anguish up to the moment of his repentance. The phrase *"my sin is always before me"* (Ps. 51:3) was not uttered in a theoretical or esoteric sense but as a genuine, profound sentiment. It was as if he could still see Uriah, full of life, saying goodbye, and later falling to the ground, bleeding, before the wall of the Ammonites, his finger pointing at David. The prolonged, anguished process of David's repentance is also expressed in Psalm 32.

The sin of David had been horrendous. Yet he had the heart of a person who had been in intimate fellowship and quiet peace with God. If an unbeliever sins, remorse may be slight or absent altogether. When believers sin, however, they will suffer deep anguish of heart because the Holy Spirit has been grieved (Eph. 4:30).

We have mentioned very little from the point of view of Bathsheba. When her husband died in battle she likely considered his death to be the result of nothing more sinister than the dangers of fighting in military campaigns. Sometime later, David, now her husband, must have confessed to her the rumors she later heard were true and that he himself had brought about Uriah's death. Imagine the enormous guilt that must have overcome the woman. Bathsheba would have to spend the rest of her life burdened by two deaths, her first husband's and her child's.

The Long-lasting Consequences

God tells David via Nathan, *"Thus says the LORD, 'Behold I will raise up adversity against you from your own house; and I will take your wives before your eyes and give them to your neighbor and he shall lie with your wives in the sight of the sun. For you did it secretly, but I will do this thing before all Israel, before the sun'"* (2 Sam. 12:11-12).

This prophecy of tremendous judgment would be literally fulfilled when David's son Absalom does exactly what had been predicted. Absalom committed this deplorable act demonstrating that the coup which he had brought about was real and that there would be no turning back. By means of this depraved deed, Absalom hoped to gain the support of the opposition; no one could harbor the smallest doubt the final line had been crossed. There would be no possibility of reconciliation. The image of Absalom on the rooftop committing these vile acts before the public bears a certain similarity to the insurrectionists and revolutionaries of our day who appear on television surrounded by high military commanders. The horror and shock they are attempting to effect is the same.

David has pronounced his own sentence. He is worthy of death and should pay four times over. The penalty of death was not imposed for the theft of an animal, but it certainly was for murder: Cursed is the one who attacks his neighbor secretly (Deut. 27:24). As a result of his actions, David would lose four sons. Absalom would kill his half-brother Amnon as a punishment for the latter's rape of Absalom's sister, Tamar (2 Sam. 13:19). Absalom is later killed by Joab's spear after he has led the nation in rebellion against David (2 Sam. 18:14). Notably David used Joab as the instrument to bring about the death of Uriah. Now the son of the king would be killed by the same man. The boomerang had returned (Gal. 6:7).

Another of David's sons, Adonijah, is killed by the order of King Solomon (1 Kgs. 2:25). In each of these cases the son's death was related to sexual sins. Amnon was killed for incest and rape (2 Sam. 13:8-14). Absalom had profaned his father's harem (2 Sam. 16:22). Adonijah sought to have as his own the woman who had in later years served as his father's concubine (Abishag, the Shunamite, 1 Kgs. 2:22).

The case of the fourth son's death is perhaps the most tragic—the child with whom Bathsheba was pregnant would not live past his infancy. With regard to the death of Bathsheba's child, Matthew Henry states, "We wonder at the sovereignty of God! The parents are the guilty ones yet they live and the child who is without fault dies. Nevertheless our souls belong to Him and He can use whatsoever means pleases Him to glorify Himself through His creatures".[2]

The principle of sin begetting death has been fulfilled (Rom. 6:23; 7:5). When we consider the royal family suffering three violent deaths and a case of incestuous rape we realize the importance of the father being an example to the children in the reverential fear of the Lord. God is not responsible for the evil acts of human beings. Nevertheless, the LORD in His providence can withdraw from men leaving them without the spiritual shield He normally uses to protect His own. Yet the Lord offers us the victory. The crippled man of Bethesda had the promise of the Lord that a victorious life is possible when He told him, *"Sin no more"* (John 5:14). This implies that it is absolutely feasible to turn away from the sin or vice that seems so difficult to overcome.

The Struggles in Our Lives

"It Just Happened"

Some may ask why this story is in the Bible, and in such detail. The answer is that God never attempts to cover up the sins of His servants. In fact, this story is recorded that we may learn from it and avoid repeating it.

H. L. Rossier states, "When we read this chapter, a sense of profound humility fills the heart of every child of God. This sin is even more serious given that it occurred in the life of a man who, in spite of his difficulties, had received the promise: *The Lord will certainly make for my lord an enduring house"* (1 Sam 25:28). He continues, "We weep at seeing the contradiction in which he trampled on the holiness of the Lord. David should have been an example of the holiness of God to the whole world!"[3]

We sometimes hear, "So and so has fallen into sin." The words suggests that the person had been doing well, spiritually speaking, and then suddenly had a totally unanticipated and tragic fall. Generally, though, spiritual failure is not an unexpected stumble but rather a progressive downward slide until one reaches the edge of the precipice. The Scriptures teach us, *"Catch us the foxes, the little foxes that spoil the vines, for our vines have tender grapes"* (Song 2:15).

Concerning this chapter of David's life, Arthur Pink writes, "This portion is very solemn. Here we see that the desires of the flesh are permitted to freely act not only in a man of the world, but also in a member of the family of faith. Here we contemplate a saint, eminent in holiness, who in a moment of neglect is surprised, seduced, and taken captive by the evil one."[4]

With all due respect to this extraordinary author, the Scriptures hint that David's fall was not instantaneous. First, the monarch was not where he should have been, as commander-in-chief at the battlefront. Likewise, when a believer is in the right place doing the right thing—engaged on the spiritual battlefield, he or she is much less likely to fall (Eph. 6:10-13).

Second, we read that David napped until nearly nightfall. We are warned in the Word of the dangers of laziness: *"now it is high time to awaken out of sleep"* (Rom. 13:11). In addition, David may have been depressed and so more easily succumbed to temptation. Our physical and emotional health greatly affect our spiritual health. God wants us to be completely healthy.

Put On the Brakes!

David had several opportunities to "put on the brakes" and avoid catastrophic consequences for himself, for his family, and even for the nation. In the words of Paul, *"Therefore let him who thinks he stands take heed lest he fall"* (1 Cor. 10:12).

The first brake that failed was David's lack of thought control at the moment he happened to see the young lady bathing. When a believer sees something that is not conducive to purity (whether on the street, on television, or in a magazine), he or she should immediately look away. The Lord Jesus Himself said, *"But I say to you that whoever looks at a woman to lust for her has already committed adultery with her in his heart"* (Matt. 5:28). What's more, He continues, *"If your right eye causes you to sin, pluck it out and cast it from you; for it is more profitable for you that one of your members perish than for your whole body to be cast into hell."*

The second brake that failed was when he began to plot how to achieve his purposes. He didn't stop to think that, with each downward step, he was essentially trampling underfoot the beautiful hymns and psalms he had written about the holiness of the Lord and our need to be faithful to Him. We also must stop-to think.

Finally, the third brake failed as well. When he inquired of his servants concerning Bathsheba and learned that she was the young wife of one of his most valiant officers (as well as the daughter of one of his captains), the audacity of his plans should have been enough to have shocked him into abandoning his

David: From the Rooftop to the Basement

lustful purposes. In order to rein in our desires, we must be able to look at ourselves honestly, so that we still can be shocked by our own sin.

Honour and Integrity

Although the majority of us will never be standing on a roof terrace in Jerusalem, equally dangerous situations abound in our present day. Internet sites that contain provocative or sexually explicit material should be absolutely off-limits for the believer. Movies, whether on TV or DVD, that are immoral in nature must be strictly avoided (1 Cor. 6:18).

Even as Bathsheba was perhaps not prudent by bathing in a place where she might be seen, in our times the believer should dress with modesty and reserve (1 Pet. 3:2-5). The Christian's manner of dress should not be provocative or a stumbling block for the opposite sex. The sons and daughters of God should not emulate fashion models or Hollywood stars, individuals who oftentimes have a disdain for purity and morality.

Be Open to the Grace of God

Eventually, David would once again pick up his harp and lift up spiritual songs in worship to the Lord. David's praise reaches unequalled heights as he sings the virtues of the One whose grace is infinite, as taken from Psalm 103.

- Who forgives all our iniquities (v. 3)
- Who redeems our life from destruction (v. 4)
- Who will not always strive with us (v. 9)
- He has not dealt with us after our iniquities nor punished us according to our sins (v. 10)

David's fall into sin has been so rapid and his scheming so wicked as to leave us astonished. Nevertheless, God's grace is greater than all of David's sins. He manifests His mercy in sending Nathan the prophet. Countless people sinking into the depths of wickedness cry out to the Lord when they at last recognize He is compassionate to the truly repentant. The message of the gospel is a message of forgiveness.

More Help Is Available to Us

Some may ask, "What hope do I have of not falling if some-one as spiritual as David fell into sin?" Today Christians have four lines of defense that David did not have.

We are the beneficiaries of the Lord's present ministry of intercession in our favor. This aspect of His ministry was not present in the times of the Old Testament (Heb. 7:25).

We have the assurance that the high priestly prayer of the Lord Jesus is being answered in our lives. *"I do not pray that You should take them out of the world, but that you should keep them from the evil one"* (John 17:15).

We possess the Holy Spirit who has been given to us (Rom. 5:5) and who leads us into all truth (John 16:13).

We have the entire canon of Scripture, the sword of the Spirit (Eph. 6:17).

For these reasons, *"we are more than conquerors"* is not simply a pleasant-sounding phrase. It is a goal which, by God's grace, we can achieve. Don't fear the fall, but rather look unto Him who can keep you from falling (Jude 24).

Using Our Gifts

Lessons for Leaders

The moral failures of the Christian in spiritual leadership have consequences reaching far beyond the individual's own life. Colleagues and fellow workers often no longer regard him or her as a godly person who inspires and leads. Among the palace staff and the servants of Bathsheba, there were undoubt-edly "a lot of little birds chirping" about what David had done.

When a leader falls in serious sin (immorality, embezzlement of ministry funds, etc.), the blessing of the Lord is lost. The only solution in these cases is total repentance before God and a full public confession. There may be some situations in which the "public" need not be extensive in scope. In no case should there be any attempt at a cover-up or a concealment of the sin.

David: From the Rooftop to the Basement

In summary, consider these points:

1. Even the most spiritual and dedicated of believers can fall into sin.

2. We must be aware of spiritual battles we will have to fight as we journey through this world.

3. It is of utmost importance to be disciplined in our lifestyles, avoiding the corrupting influences often prevalent on television, the Internet, and the movies.

4. God completely forgives sin, but the consequences of sin can be prolonged and very painful. For this reason the apostle John says, *"My little children, I am writing these things to you that you may not sin"* (1 John 2:1).

5. Confession and disclosure are of utmost importance. God is able to forgive even the most serious of sins but they must be confessed. *"If we confess our sins, God is faithful and righteous to forgive our sins and to cleanse us from all unrighteousness"* (1 John 1:9).

Real Heroes

Uriah and Nathan the prophet are the true spiritual leaders in this story. The military officer demonstrated unflinching loyalty and dedication. He died a hero.

The prophet confronted the king with incredible courage and wisdom. Doubtless, Nathan had been in the presence of the Lord, who had shown him exactly what to say and how to say it.

The grace of God sustains all of us and, in fact, restores us when we fall. Another prophet, Jeremiah, expressed this beautifully: *"Through the LORD'S mercies we are not consumed, Because His compassions fail not. They are new every morning; Great is Your faithfulness"* (Lam. 3:22-23).

Comparison, Contrast and Ideas for Expansion

(As if a theatrical play, in this story each principal character has an important decision to make. Like a house of cards, when the first card falls the others fall with it). Six consecutive decisions.

1. David decides to invite Bathsheba to dine with him
2. Bathsheba accepts the invitation
3. Uriah does not return to his house, contrary to the plotting of the king.
4. Uriah again sleeps only at the gate of the palace.
5. The king decides Uriah must die on the battlefield.
6. Joab decides to obey the criminal order of the king.

This story may be divided into five distinct messages, probably sent either verbally or by means of letters.

1. David to Bathsheba: an invitation to the palace
2. Bathsheba to David: a short message, "I have a problem."
3. David to Joab: a letter, "Send Uriah to me."
4. David to Joab: a written communication to commit a crime, "Put Uriah in the most dangerous place."
5. Joab to David: a coded message to inform the king that his objective had been accomplished.

Contrasts between Jezebel and David (concerning the Bathsheba episode)

Jezebel	David
Was Queen	Was King
Did not regard highly the law of God	Did not regard highly the law of God
Sent a letter	Sent a letter
Had accomplices (false witnesses)	Had an accomplice (Joab)
Naboth died because he was upright	Uriah died because he was upright

David: From the Rooftop to the Basement

Jezebel	David
Jezebel killed a just man	David killed a just man
A prophet denounces her	A prophet denounces him

Discussion Starters

1. What are the similarities and differences among the terms *sin, temptation, falsehood,* and *repentance?*

2. At what points in the biblical story could the "chain reaction" of sin been broken?

3. Describe Uriah's sense of responsibility and commitment. Give examples.

4. What responsibility did Bathsheba have in all of this?

5. What are the qualities of God's forgiveness, as described in Psalms 32 and 51?

Chapter 3

DAVID: COUNTING PEOPLE...
BUT NOT THE COST

All of Judah's military leaders, including of course General Joab, have come together by order of the king. In the great hall of the palace there is a certain uneasiness. Why did King David convene the meeting?

Does a Census Make Sense?

Presenting the "Need"

David steps into the chamber. He is no longer the impetuous youth who had defeated Goliath. Neither is he the same handsome man whose sophisticated charm seduced the wife of Uriah. The years have passed and the king has grayed. The furrowed lines of his face reveal the effects of the passing years and the burdens of life.

The sovereign looks around the room and then speaks, "Gentlemen, the reason for this meeting is that we have a serious problem. The fact is, we simply do not know our military potential. Ambassadors and kings from neighboring countries have visited me and told of their military prowess. They know precisely how many war chariots they possess. They have detailed lists of their cavalry soldiers and can cite the exact number of men in their infantry. I realize the figures are likely exaggerated; these minor nations simply cannot have such large armies.

"But it shames me and embarrasses me that when I am asked about the size of our military, I simply don't know what to say. In fact, one of the visiting rulers who could not restrain himself gave me a mocking smile. Clearly it is not proper that a great nation such as ours would not know how many soldiers we have. I believe it is in the national interest to determine the precise numbers of our military strength.

"I hereby order that a census be conducted!"

"Your Majesty," says the commander in chief, "If you will permit me a word."

"Proceed," responds the king impatiently.

"May the LORD make His people a hundred times more than they are. But, my lord the king, are they not all my lord's servants? Why then does my lord require this thing? Why should he be a cause of guilt in Israel?" (1 Chron. 21:3).

A silence falls upon the assembly. Then a battle-experienced veteran of high rank rises and asks to speak. "My King, I must say that I am in agreement with the counsel of General Joab. You well know the LORD promised to Abraham to multiply his descendants until they were a people as the sand of the seas. If we census the nation, it would be as if we had no trust in God's Word. You certainly know that there has never been a census since we came to possess the land which God has given us."

King David grows angry. His face reddens. With a loud and barely controlled voice, he says, "My captains and generals, I'm grateful for your opinion. And the things that you have said, I know very well. But I am the one in charge!" His voice grows somber and he says, "Whoever fails to immediately implement my orders will at once be removed from his position."

The military chiefs beg forgiveness and respectfully dismiss themselves.

David: Counting People...but Not the Cost

The Count Begins

In the subsequent months the officers go throughout the nation conducting a military census. The goal: to determine how many soldiers could be enlisted in time of war. Finally, the official results are tallied and the numbers calculated. In Israel, there are 800,000 men who can use the sword; in Judah, 500,000.

More months pass, and it is obvious that the well-being of the nation has suffered. King David realizes that the timing of this bad state of affairs is no mere coincidence. The nation has begun to feel the effects of his sin. *"And God was displeased with this thing; therefore He struck Israel"* (1 Chron. 21:7).

King David is distressed. He well knows that he has done wrong in ordering the census. Additionally, he has neglected to impose the minimal census tax dictated by the Law of Moses. He realizes that failure to do so carries the divine discipline of a plague. As the days pass the situation worsens. He begins to feel as if his heart were buffeting him. At length he comes to the end of himself and finally goes to the Lord in prayer. *"I have sinned greatly because I have done this thing; but now, I pray, take away the iniquity of Your servant, for I have done very foolishly"* (1 Chron. 21:8).

The afternoon and night pass without a response. David feels that God has not heard him. The following morning, an attendant informs the king that Gad the prophet has asked for a word with him. The man of God enters the king's chamber and greets him respectfully but without undue flattery. His face reveals seriousness and sadness, bringing an air of drama to the scene.

Numbering the Consequences

A Message from God

"My king," says the prophet, "I have a message from God for you."

David grows pale. His voice trembles as he asks, "Please, what is the message?"

"The Lord has determined your sentence," responds Gad. "He offers you three choices."

A deathly silence comes over the room; David can feel his heart pounding. "What are the choices that are given to me?"

The prophet Gad answers in a resolute voice, the words bearing the force of a hammer blow. *"three years of famine"* (1 Chron. 21:12).

David's face becomes even more pale. The king well knows the ramifications of famine. He has heard the shocking accounts of inhuman acts committed by people who are enduring starvation during times of siege. He cannot imagine a place where children no longer play in the streets because hunger saps their spirits. He cannot picture his people desperately scrounging the fields and waste areas in search of the tiniest morsel of food. The famine will prostrate his proud army. He shakes his head, "No, no!"

The second hammer blow falls: *"or three months to be defeated by your foes with the sword of your enemies overtaking you,"* (1 Chron. 21:12).

The duration of the punishment has been reduced from three years to only three months. But three months of defeat in battle and retreating from a vanquishing enemy is too much to contemplate. Again the face of the king grows somber. He has seen battlefields after the fighting has ceased, filled with bodies of the dead and the fatally wounded. Again the monarch shakes his head. "No! May it not be! Please, what is the final choice?"

The final hammer blow falls. *"Or else for three days the sword of the Lord—the plague in the land, with the angel of the Lord destroying throughout all the territory of Israel."* The prophet pauses then says, *"Now consider what answer I should take back to Him who sent me"* (1 Chron. 21:12).

The King Chooses

David's face reflects the pain in his heart. He knows that his sin has brought serious judgment on his people, and he is truly repentant. The king answers, *"I am in great distress. Please let me fall into the hand of the Lord, for His mercies are very great; but do not let me fall into the hand of man."* (1 Chron. 21:14).

Gad nods his understanding—David has chosen the third punishment—and leaves the monarch. *"So the Lord sent a plague upon Israel, and seventy thousand men of Israel fell"* (1 Chron. 21:15).

In every town and city, people were sick and dying. One man's sin had brought pain to the entire country. But there was more. The wave of disease that had swelled outside the capital was now drawing closer to the walls of the city. The multitudes of the city's residents pray for deliverance. King David went up to the roof, where he can see the angel of destruction in the distance, smiting the people with pestilence. David is desperate and fears that the population of the city of Jerusalem will be decimated. In anguish he cries out to God: *"I am the one who has sinned and done evil indeed; but these sheep, what have they done? Let Your hand, I pray, O Lord my God, be against me and my father's house, but not against Your people that they should be plagued"* (1 Chron. 21:17).

Gad hastens to King David and instructs him to rush to the threshing floor of Ornan the Jebusite and to build an altar to the Lord there. The ruler hurries to obey. Smoke from the sacrifices wisps upward into the sky. David's voice cries out in prayer. Suddenly, the Lord commands the destroying angel to cease: *"It is enough; now restrain your hand"* (1 Chron. 21:15).

The angel returns the sword to its sheath and then disappears. David realizes how God had answered and delivered His people. The king declares that this will be the place to worship and make sacrifices to God. (At that time the tabernacle and altar were at *"the high place in Gibeon"* (1 Chron. 21:29), rather than in the holy city of Jerusalem). On that spot the temple, the house of the LORD God would be built.

Our Struggle with Good & Evil
The Bible Back-Story

What's the Difference?

We must approach these sacred pages with reverence. What had begun as a single sin has borne a devastating chain of consequences. The Lord is angry with His people. Although not part of the narrative that we have considered, the Scriptures inform us that God permitted Satan to incite David to sin. As a result, a national tragedy occurs with seventy thousand dying in a plague. If the story had ended there, it would be a very sad one.

There are three questions which we must ask:

1. What does it mean that Satan incited David to sin?
2. Why did the entire nation suffer for the sin of one man?
3. Was the judgment overly severe?

There is a difference between the census numbers as recorded in 2 Samuel and the results mentioned in 1 Chronicles. Some believe that 2 Samuel 24:9 does not count the regular army of 280,000 soldiers (1 Chron. 27:1-15) and the numbers are rounded.[1]

Others note that the 2 Samuel reports the number of *"valiant men who drew the sword"* while in 1 Chronicles mention is made simply of those *"who drew the sword."*

Kings, presidents, and other prominent people make decisions that may affect everyone. It is probable that the ambition to undertake a military invasion of neighboring nations was in the mind of King David. If had taken place, perhaps more than seventy thousand soldiers would have been killed, that is, more than the number who died in the plague.

Incited to Sin?

"Now Satan stood up against Israel and moved David to number Israel" (1 Chron. 21:1). The word *incite* could be understood as instigating the king to do something seriously wrong. The ruler, due to the spiritual state in which he found himself, was susceptible to doing things he would never have done when he

walked closely with the Lord. David is a man who has ascended to the heights of fellowship with God and service to the Lord. In this account, however, we are considering one of the lowest moments of his life. For this reason the apostle warns us, *"Be sober; be vigilant; because your adversary the devil walks about like a roaring lion, seeking whom he may devour"* (1 Pet. 5:8).

The wicked one is always attacking the people of God. It seems that David had put himself in a spiritually vulnerable position. When we are no longer under God's protection the results can be catastrophic. The Lord Jesus said to Peter, *"Simon! Simon! Indeed, Satan has asked for you that he may sift you as wheat. But I have prayed for you, that your faith should not fail"* (Luke 22:31-32).

An Entire Nation Suffers

First, David sinned in seeking to number the people. The ancient historian Josephus (b. AD 37) suggests that the sin consisted in not exacting the small tribute (half shekel) required by the law at a time of census. *"When you take the census of the children of Israel for their number, then every man shall give a ransom for himself to the LORD, when you number them, that there may be no plague among them when you number them"* (Ex. 30:12).

Second, by taking a census, King David demonstrated a lack of faith in the promise given to Abraham to multiply your descendants as the stars of the heaven and as the sand which is on the seashore (Gen. 22:17). Obviously by determining the number of men fit for war, the military might of the nation was clearly demonstrated, tantamount to a declaration of national pride.

Nevertheless, the judgment of God did not fall upon a nation that caused no guilt on sin. God has only once sentenced an individual who was absolutely innocent and this was His Holy Son (2 Cor. 5:21). David did say, *"I have sinned greatly because I have done this thing; but now, I pray, take away the iniquity of Your servant, for I have done very foolishly"* (1 Chron. 21:8). In the Old Testament, however, the leaders always took full responsibility for the actions of their people even though the rulers were not necessarily the ones primarily to blame.

Scripture does declare that the Lord's anger was incited against Israel; no mention is made of David. We might suppose the source of anger was the attitude of discontentment on the part of the people toward the authority of God manifested in the king. John Gill, quoting Kimchi, proposes two areas in which the iniquity of the people may be observed:

1. **The rebellion of Absalom.** Many had followed after this worldly and proud young man. *"And the conspiracy grew strong, for the people with Absalom continually increased in number"* (2 Sam. 15:12).

2. **The uprising of Sheba.** *"And he blew a trumpet, and said: 'We have no share in David, nor do we have inheritance in the son of Jesse…' So every man of Israel deserted David, and followed Sheba the son of Bichri"* (2 Sam 20:1-2a).[2]

Was God Overly Severe?

God is absolutely just. In determining a punishment for sin, He never disciplines neither more or less than what is proper; His justice and His grace go hand in glove. How comforting it is for us to know that *"the Judge of all the earth, will He not do right?"* (Gen. 18:25).

God gave King David a choice among three distinct punishments. This opportunity was unusual and presented the king with a difficult decision. With the chosen punishment, that of plague, there was a much greater possibility that he and his family would suffer as well. Yet David trusted in the mercy of the Lord. Matthew Henry comments, "The hunger and the sword will devour in the same manner the one as the other, but it can be imagined that the destroying angel would use his sword against those who were known by God to be the most guilty."[3]

The Struggles in Our Lives

How sad it is that David had forgotten that the reason he defeated Goliath was not his own strength. He had forgotten that, even though Saul sought him with an army five times greater than his own, Saul was never able to lay a finger on him because God was with him (1 Sam. 24:2). Let us not forget our own histories with God's grace and power.

God in His grace forgives our sins when we are truly repentant, just as He did with David. The one who is truly contrite will not repeat the sins but instead will find strength in the grace of God. *"He who covers his sins will not prosper, but whoever confesses and forsakes them will have mercy"* (Prov. 28:13). Disobedience, however, is not without its consequences. God is most certainly ready to forgive, but the effects of sin can leave scars that are deep and painful.

Since His ascension, Jesus our Saviour now has a ministry of intercession as our advocate because *"He always lives to make intercession for them"* (Heb 7:25). Our advocate for the defense has never lost a case, yet no Scripture indicates that Jesus exercised this ministry prior to His incarnation. Thus we see that David did not enjoy the marvellous protection that is the privilege of the believer in our times.

In the spiritual sense, our Lord was He who would receive the blows of the sword. *"Awake, O sword, against My Shepherd, against the Man who is My companion"* (Zech. 13:7). In the same place where the angel stood *"between heaven and earth, with his sword unsheathed"* (1 Chron 21:16), the son of David would build the temple of Jerusalem. In that same temple, *"On the last day, that great day of the feast, Jesus stood and cried out, saying, 'If anyone thirsts, let him come to Me and drink. He who believes in Me, as the Scripture has said, out of his heart will flow rivers of living water'"* (John 7:37-38).

The book of 2 Samuel ends on a note of liberation and blessing. Hertzberg compares this chapter with the Genesis flood and says, "new blessings come as a consequence of punishment and destruction"[4]

Using Our Gifts

As a leader David took complete responsibility for the well-being of his people. He assumes the blame for the Lord's anger.

He does not justify himself by pleading ignorance but rather freely and clearly confesses his fault.

In our day there is a tendency to think that we can sin and suffer no consequences. Mistakenly, we ask forgiveness from the LORD with the attitude that all will be well and we begin the cycle all over again. Instead, let us resolve to respond to the voice of conscience as soon as it convicts us.

Discussion Starters

1. What different views of the importance of fulfilling God's commandments do we see in this account?

2. What is true repentance?

3. What specific evidence of the grace of God is there in this event in David's life?

4. How has the Lord interceded on your behalf?

Chapter 4

SOLOMON: ARCHITECT AND WORSHIPPER

The bright sun rose against the clear sky. Thousands and thousands of people have gathered in front of the imposing edifice. The beautifully adorned columns positioned at the front of the temple are both majestic and imposing.

The Temple

Grand Opening

Suddenly the joyful notes of trumpets, cymbals, and flutes fill the air, heightening the anticipation of the crowd. It appears that the entire city has come out for the great celebration. The long-awaited day has come at last.

Among the multitudes who have arrived in Jerusalem from the nearby villages stands a small child, clinging to his father's hand and looking curiously around him. "Daddy, why are all these people so happy?"

The father, who himself is smiling, answers, "Today is the dedication of the temple. The King of all our people is going to preside over its opening. "

"Daddy, what is a temple?"

His father patiently responds, "Well, I'm not sure how best to explain it to you. It is like an enormous house where the Lord lives. Our Lord is very great." Then his thoughts go beyond the simple question, and he continues, "God is so immense that the heavens themselves cannot contain Him. Somehow, the Lord will dwell in this temple. Our God will be here with us, right here in the middle of Jerusalem. From now on we will be well protected because the Lord is going to be so close. Whatever happens to us, we can come here and He will take care of us."

"Daddy, if the temple is so good, why didn't we have one before?"

The father grows quiet as he ponders the question. His eyes fill with tears. As the two continue to walk toward the temple, the songs of praise and the sound of the instruments grow stronger and more emphatic.

The great courtyard In front of the massive building has been filled with the congregating multitudes. Hundreds of priests, their robes immaculately white, have already taken up their stations. A procession enters, reciting Psalm 136: "Oh, give thanks to the LORD, for He is good!" The crowd responds in unison: "For His mercy endures forever."

Lines of the psalm sound forth again: *"To Him who alone does great wonders…"* (Ps. 136:4). As each verse is announced, more voices join in response. Now thousands cry out the refrain: *"For His mercy endures forever"* (Ps. 136:4).

In the middle of the huge esplanade stands a finely crafted bronze platform. The officials of state accompany the king as he approaches it. The crowds shout with enthusiasm, "Long live the king!" The instruments, trumpets, tambourines, horns, and cymbals, are played again with such fervor they seem to shake the very walls of the city.

The monarch walks slowly and with the dignity befitting his office. On his head rests the royal crown; his garments are of the finest linen. A sash embellished with threads of gold adorns his chest. The generals of the army follow the king in an orderly procession toward to the platform. The ministers of state, all finely dressed, are the last to proceed.

The House of God

With great solemnity, the priests bear the Ark of the Covenant into the Most Holy place. All stand in awe as a cloud fills the house of the LORD (1 Kgs. 8:10). As the sovereign ascends the bronze platform, absolute silence falls upon the crowd. The king looks across the assembled masses and then speaks, with a voice strong, resolute, and clear, *"The LORD said He would dwell in the dark cloud. I have surely built You an exalted house, and a place for You to dwell in forever"* (2 Chron. 6:1-2).

King Solomon turns around, blesses the whole assembly of Israel, and then bows down. Humbly kneeling before the LORD, he prays, *"LORD God of Israel, there is no God in heaven or on earth like You, who keep Your covenant and mercy with Your servants who walk before You with all their hearts… But will God indeed dwell with men on the earth? Behold, heaven and the heaven of heavens cannot contain You. How much less this temple which I have built!"* (2 Chron. 6:14, 18).

The king continues his lengthy prayer, emphasizing God's greatness, humanity's lowliness, and the incongruity of God dwelling among people. Solomon asks for mercy if the people should fall into sin or a crisis beset them. He prays that the Lord will hear the voice of the people, forgive them, and work among them. *"Now, my God, I pray, let Your eyes be open and let Your ears be attentive to the prayer made in this place"* (2 Chron. 6:40). When Solomon had finished praying, fire came down from heaven and consumed the burnt offering and the sacrifices, and the glory of the LORD filled the temple.

The people are astonished and quickly bow their faces to the ground. The spectacle has been both wondrous and frightening. Never before had the people seen the glory of the LORD. The great celebration continues for fourteen days, and then the people return to their homes. Among them is the father with his son. "Daddy, I saw the fire fall from heaven and I saw the Lord's glory!"

"Son, never forget what you saw. Stay faithful to God all your life."

Sometime later, the Lord appears to Solomon. *"I have heard your prayer and have chosen this place for myself as a house of sacrifice. When I shut up heaven and there is no rain or command the locusts to devour the land or send pestilence among My people, if My people who are called by My name will humble themselves and pray and seek My face and turn from their wicked ways then I will hear from heaven and will forgive their sin and heal their land. Now My eyes will be open and My ears attentive to prayer made in this place"* (2 Chron. 7:12-15).

An Extraordinary Woman

Solomon and the IQ Test

The fame of Solomon spread far and wide and caught the attention of the Queen of Sheba. She decides to visit him in Jerusalem.

Extensive and lavish preparations have been made throughout the kingdom. The arrival of the distinguished guest is preceded by soldiers mounted on black horses and bearing spears and shields glistening with colors of the realm. The mounted warriors are followed by a seemingly endless stream of chariots carrying the high dignitaries of Sheba. In the midst of this impressive procession is the queen's own chariot. The royal conveyance is surrounded by riders mounted on white horses and wearing brilliantly adorned helmets with colorful feathered crests.

King Solomon himself directs the reception ceremony. His opulent throne, worthy of display in a fine arts museum, is located in a commanding position above the court. The throne is of the finest marble, completely overlaid with pure gold. The supports of the armrests have been sculpted in the form of an attacking lion. The footstool has seven steps; on each side is carved a golden statue of a lion fashioned as if ready to attack anyone who would dare offend the royal authority.

Solomon: Architect and Worshipper

The rays of the morning sun enter through the high, narrow windows of the palace, creating a burnished golden halo glimmering around the footstool. Seated on the throne, the king is resplendent in his regal apparel and ornately decorated crown. On either side he is flanked by generals, ministers, and men of high religious positions attired in their finest ceremonial robes.

The Queen Arrives

Heralds announce the arrival of the queen with blaring trumpets. The Queen of Sheba has visited many foreign courts but never had a reception so majestic and compelling.

After a time of long salutations and the many speeches commensurate with royal protocol, the feasting begins. The queen is left nearly speechless. The delicacies lavishly covering the dining tables are exquisite beyond words. There is an abundance of gourmet specialties from all the neighboring nations, prepared by masters of the gastronomic art. The utensils and goblets are plated with the finest gold and encrusted with precious stones. The queen is astonished by how the entire event proceeds with precision and perfect organization.

The following day the king takes his visitor on a tour of the city. The official entourage pauses before the temple of the Lord. Standing in awe before the enormous and gloriously detailed edifice, the queen gazes at it with wonderment. The sight of the imposing structure produces a profound emotional effect. She has seen many temples. Some have been large and some have been elaborate, but this one has something distinct which none of the others have had. She senses something special about it, something inexpressible.

"Your Majesty," says the queen, "would it be possible to enter the temple?"

"I am very sorry," responds Solomon. "Only the High Priest may enter the Holiest Place and he only once a year. Even I am not permitted to enter there."

Finally the day arrives on which the purpose of the royal visitor will be satisfied. The queen will definitely and finally decide if the fame that surrounds Solomon is based on reality or is merely a façade. Before beginning her journey, the queen had taken counsel from the most trusted advisors of her kingdom as to questions to pose to the king. She now presents them to him—questions dealing with astronomy, biology, and botany. One by one the king answers the questions, never hesitating and always responding correctly, even to the most difficult questions.

The queen is fascinated not only by the wisdom of Solomon as a man but by the greatness and splendors of his kingdom. She contemplates the vestments and the habitations of the king's officials. The officers of Solomon's court are more exquisitely clothed than even some kings whom she has known. She later proclaims these immortal words: *"It was a true report which I heard in my own land about your words and your wisdom. However I did not believe their words until I came and saw with my own eyes; and indeed the half of the greatness of your wisdom was not told me. You exceed the fame of which I heard"* (2 Chron. 9:5-6).

The queen returns to her own land. She will never forget the wonders she has seen. King Solomon has shown her majestic buildings and splendid treasures. Above all, the memory of the king's simple but profound faith in the God of Israel stays with her.

The Bible Back-Story

Who Was Solomon?

The inauguration of the temple marked the high point in the life of Solomon—not because of the physical greatness of the building but rather from the perspective of Solomon's spiritual life. Solomon never had any great battle victories to celebrate. There were no processions of hundreds of chained prisoners being marched before the populace in a demonstration of his prowess and exploits. But Solomon enjoyed the moment of this triumphant spiritual victory.

Solomon: Architect and Worshipper

Solomon was the tenth son of King David (1 Chron. 3:5), who had promised him the kingdom by divine command (1 Chron. 28:5). Following the death of David, Solomon astutely managed the political and social affairs of Israel to avoid the dangers of a civil war erupting. He moved quickly to eliminate or negate his rivals and those whom he did not consider allies. His half-brother Adonijah (1 Kgs. 3:25) headed up the sad line of people who marched toward death by the thirsty sword of Benaniah, Solomon's commander. Adonijah was followed by the famous ex-commander of the army of Israel, Joab (1 Kgs. 2:24). Afterwards Shimei, of the dynasty of Saul, was executed as well (1 Kgs. 3:46). The only rival who was spared, though condemned never to leave the walls of the city (perhaps a house arrest?), was the high priest Abiathar (1 Kgs. 2:27).

The purges were realized at the military, religious, and political levels. Solomon had no reservations concerning the drastic decisions to be made, some of which we would consider to be cruel, such as ordering the death of his half-brother. Solomon had learned the bitter lesson of civil war when his half-brother Absalom precipitated an insurrection against his father (2 Sam. 15:12). Later, Solomon's son Rehoboam would describe him by saying, *"My father made your yoke heavy"* and that he *"chastised the people with whips"* (2 Chron. 10:14).

Interestingly, as Rehoboam is speaking with the people, he is advised by his father's counselors to moderate the policy of his father's harsh rule—wise counsel indeed (although Rehoboam did not heed it). Thus we see that in spite of all of his personal wisdom, Solomon still had need of other counselors and often he should have listened to them.

Notice Solomon's references to himself in his prayer: *"I have fulfilled the position of my father...sit on the throne...I have built the temple"* (2 Chron. 6:10). Solomon does not take advantage of the moment for self-aggrandizement or abuse the words of his prayer, but neither does he fail to make mention of himself.

Instead of being a great military leader as was generally expected of the kings of those times, Solomon was an avid student of nature, what we might call an earth scientist or a biologist. He was also widely recognized for the great public works he undertook during the days of his reign. In addition Solomon was well known as a writer, poet, and philosopher. He was what we would regard today as a "Renaissance man." Perhaps the only thing lacking is outstanding musical ability, which his father, David, possessed.

We see Solomon as a great poet in the Song of Solomon, a true literary jewel. Proverbs displays Solomon's skill not only as a writer but also as an observer of human nature, a forerunner of what we might now call a sociologist. In that book, Solomon shows that he has carefully observed and examined the various facets of life and come to understand a great deal concerning human personality and behavior (psychology). In Proverbs, Solomon writes of the rich, the poor, the avaricious, the lazy, "easy women," factious men, the just, and the wicked. In the Book of Ecclesiastes we see Solomon the philosopher. In spite of all his riches and political might, his pleasure-filled life leads him to conclude that, under the sun, *"all is vanity and grasping for the wind"* (Eccl. 1:14).

King Solomon was a man who had much. Had he lived in modern times he might well have won the Nobel Prize for his knowledge of biology and the Pulitzer Prize for his works of literature. He was not a great warrior, but he was a man of outstanding knowledge and wisdom.

The construction of the great temple of Solomon began in approximately 967 BC, during the fourth year of his reign. The completion of the building would require seven years. The festivities surrounding the dedication of the temple were extensive and the sacrifices offered were staggering: 22,000 bulls and 120,000 sheep. Although Solomon plainly declared that any man-made temple would be totally unable to contain the God of heaven, his prayer seems to indicate that the temple was such an extraordinary architectural work that God would inhabit it forever (2 Chron. 6:1). In the New Testament, the Lord Jesus declares that God would dwell with His own and that His people would be His spiritual temple: *"If anyone loves Me, he*

Solomon: Architect and Worshipper

will keep My word; and My Father will love him, and We will come to him and make Our home with him" (John 14:23).

By ancient standards, the temple of Solomon was not destined to endure for long. In contrast, Jesus Christ, who said that something *"greater than Solomon is here"* (Matt. 12:42), is a *"temple"* that He Himself raised up and which will endure forever (Heb. 7:13).

The Queen and Her Questions

It may well be that the Queen of Sheba questioned Solomon concerning concrete matters of a scientific, political, and administrative nature. Scholars tell us that the Hebrew term in this text signifies puzzling questions, enigmas, or riddles. This includes profound philosophical, practical, and theological matters. Arabic literature of the time abounds with enigmas and puzzles.[1]

The Jamieson-Fausset-Brown Bible Commentary cites an interesting extra-biblical legend of an occasion when Solomon was in his garden with all the officials of his court. Unexpectedly, the Queen of Sheba, who was standing somewhat apart from the others, pulled out a beautiful bouquet of flowers and showed them to everyone present. She kept her distance from the others so that they could not determine whether the flowers had a pleasing fragrance. The queen asked Solomon if the flowers were real or artificial. According to the legend, the king looked at the bouquet of flowers and at first seemed perplexed and hesitant. Suddenly the king noticed some bees buzzing around some nearby wildflowers. The king's countenance brightened and a smile appeared on his lips. He commanded that the bouquet of flowers be placed near the wall where the wildflowers were growing. A few moments later he had the answer. The bees had not approached the queen's flowers. The king arose and confidently declared, "Those flowers are a wonderful work of art but they are not real." Those assembled applauded loudly; Solomon had again demonstrated his wisdom.[2]

Interestingly, the wisdom of Solomon was most famously demonstrated by his interactions with three women (the two mothers of Chapter 5 and the Queen of Sheba). In my opinion, greater emphasis on and reference to women is found in the life of Solomon than those of the other kings of Israel and Judah.

Sheba corresponds to what is today known as Yemen in the Arabian Peninsula. The queen's visit likely included discussion of practical aspects in establishing and developing commerce between the two nations. The mission also may have dealt with permission for the safe transit of caravans and merchandise as well as the use of some ports in Israel.

David had predicted that to the "Son of the King" would be given the gold of Sheba (Ps. 72:15). While a partial completion of the prophecy occurred in the days of Solomon, the true fulfillment yet awaits the establishment of the millennial reign of Christ.

The Struggles in Our Lives

An Amazing Prayer

In his words before the temple, Solomon declares that the Lord fulfilled His promise by His own hand (2 Chron. 6:15) but that blessings and answered prayer are not unconditional. The people are solemnly warned that if they abandon the statutes of God and give themselves to idolatry, they will be carried away into captivity and the beautiful temple will be destroyed. We too must listen to God and be diligent in what He expects of us.

We can learn much from the form and content of Solomon's prayer because it underscores many of the attributes of God: **He is incomparable,** *"LORD God of Israel, there is no God in heaven or on earth like You"* (2 Chron. 6:14); **He is faithful,** *"You have kept what You promised Your servant David"* (2 Chron. 6:15); and **He is infinite and immeasurable,** *"Behold, heaven and the heaven of heavens cannot contain You"* (2 Chron. 6:18).

The temple prayer also is instructive because of its sincerity, earnestness, and genuine humility. It is also consistent and continuous. Just as a chorus in a musical repeats a refrain, Solomon reiterates the same basic supplication following each point of prayer: *"Then hear from heaven and forgive the sin of Your people Israel, and bring them back to the land which You gave to them and their fathers"* (2 Chron. 6:25, 27, 30, 33, 39, 45). Finally, we should emulate the king's prayer in 2 Chronicles 6 because it is very specific, citing the case of a legal dispute with no witnesses; military defeat; drought; famine, blight, and pestilence; foreigners (Gentiles) in need; soldiers on the battlefield in foreign lands; and divine judgment upon the people as a result of their disobedience.

Glory and Honour

Although these events literally took place, the story is replete with images and phrases that elevate us to things far greater than that particular time and place. The experiences of the Queen of Sheba have many parallels to those of the believer in Jesus Christ. In addition, the symbol of Solomon prefigures Christ in His glory.

The queen had carefully considered the grandeur of the royal palace, the abundance of rich food on the table, the elegant clothing of the king's officials, and the formal and stately procession of the priests of the Lord. She was awed by the immensity and extent of the splendors of Solomon's reign. The queen's exclamation of wonder resounds with feeling that goes beyond Solomon. These very words found their way into innumerable hymns describing the One who is *"Chief among ten thousand"* (Song 5:10).

As the ruler over a prosperous territory, the Queen of Sheba possessed great riches; indeed, she brought many valuable gifts for the king. She presented to him a wealth of aromatic spices, gold in abundance, and precious gems. The scene brings to mind the description of the arrival of the Magi shortly after the birth of the Lord Jesus (Matt. 2:11).

Nevertheless, she was most amazed by Solomon's wisdom and realized that to be in his presence, to hear him, and to learn of his wisdom was marvellous indeed. Similarly, the fundamental way we are blessed is not by fancy clothing, expensive homes, or the like but by the high honour and privilege of hearing the wisdom of the true King. At the end of our journey, we will see not only the heavenly Jerusalem but also the Lord Jesus in His glory (Rev. 1:13-18). We will then pour out our hearts in praise when we understand those things that were incomprehensible to us on this side of the river (Rom. 8:18).

The day came when the Queen of Sheba had to return to her own realm. She had to leave the splendors of Jerusalem and would no longer hear and be amazed by Solomon's wise sayings and proverbs. The queen however, had learned much during her sojourn, even about the everlasting love of the Lord for Israel. She also had received from the King of Israel presents in accord with his great generosity—all she desired, whatever she asked, and much more than she had brought to the king. She was grateful, just as we should be. Our Saviour is generous with us far beyond what we could ever request (John 14:13-14; 16:23; Eph. 1:3; 3:20).

Using Our Gifts

Receiving the Torch

Important aspects of leadership ability can be seen in the building projects of Solomon, not only in the construction of the temple but also in lesser works. He begins one work after another but sees each one through to completion. In contrast, there are many in this world whose undertakings resemble Schubert's *Unfinished Symphony*.

In his prayer and discourse, Solomon repeats the phase *"my father David"*. He may well have wanted to communicate that he alone was the legitimate heir to the throne, but he certainly wanted to celebrate that he was realizing the golden dream of the great King David. Solomon's father had amassed an enormous quantity of materials to be used in the temple's construction including gold, silver, and precious stones (1 Chron. 29:2). Nevertheless the success of such an enterprise depended on innumerable workers (managers, architects, artisans, metallurgists, sculptors, and others). The use of construction materials as well as the management of personnel required wise and careful administration.

Israel was not an advanced society; its economy was based primarily on agriculture and commerce. It would certainly have been difficult to find in the country sufficient artisans with the required skills for the enormity of the enterprise. Nevertheless the Lord always provides whatever is necessary to see His works accomplished.

Her Majesty

In this biblical story we learn not only about a remarkable female leader, the Queen of Sheba, but also that King Solomon in no way regretted the time he spent answering her questions. He recognized her exceptional intelligence and education. In fact, Josephus wrote that it was the custom of those days to hold a sort of intellectual contest between persons of importance.

Initially the queen was both curious about and skeptical of Solomon. She had heard much about him and, while not naively accepting all that she heard, neither did she reject the stories. She serves as a model for us: when faced with the new and perhaps questionable, we should inquire and investigate.

As a leader the queen knew when and how to use praise; her speech shows that she was articulate and cultured. Her education and training were unusual for women of that era unless they were of the nobility or of the highest class (politically, religiously, or militarily). A leader is a teacher and an example and must be tactful, especially in difficult situations. For example, the Queen of Sheba reminded Solomon that God had given him all he had, not so that he could enjoy an opulent lifestyle, but so that he could *"do justice and righteousness"* (2 Chron. 9:9). This principle is applicable to the Christian leader in our times as well.

In the ancient world, a journey of 1,400 miles was difficult under the best of conditions, but the queen accepted the challenge. Today's Christian leader also must be willing to undertake journeys, whether literal or figurative, that can be arduous and even dangerous.

Discussion Starters

1. Describe the social and spiritual situations that Solomon sets forth in his prayer and relate those to the conditions found in today's world.

2. What are the conditions for receiving the blessings of God?

3. How did the Queen of Sheba exemplify one who is truly seeking the truth and the purpose of life?

Chapter 5

SOLOMON: THE WISE AND FOOLISH KING

The Lie Detector

The king gives a terse order and the executioner, with deep reluctance, raises his sharpened sword high over his head. Although the hard-bitten man is accustomed to cold-heartedly executing criminals, at this moment his eyes are filled with tears of pity and compassion. Never had there been done what the king was now ordering him to do. His razor sharp sword had many times fallen on criminals with herculean force. But this time was different, very different.

Two Mothers, Two Babies

On top of the wooden table before him lay a newborn babe. The child had been tied down with cords. The little boy twists and struggles to change position as if he understood what was happening. His little body is unblemished, the tiny fingers of his hands and the toes of his feet are perfect. His face seems to be a sculpture by Michelangelo.

But the command to prepare to kill the child has been given and the executioner apprehensively holds the heavy instrument ready to divide the child into two equal pieces. In a few moments, the thrashing arms and legs will be stilled forever. The king, seated on an ornately decorated bench, seems detached and impenetrable. He reveals no emotion whatsoever as he prepares to give the final order of execution. Those who are present are appalled and revolted by the scene and stand in disgusted horror. Many have closed their eyes.

It had all begun days before. Two women of "ill-repute" had given birth to their respective boys within three days of one another. Not even the women themselves were sure who the fathers of their children were. Both of these women lived under the same roof and in that house there was but one bed which both women shared. During the night, one of the women rolled on top of her newborn, smothering him.

The next morning the woman who had inadvertently smothered her son awoke and noticed that her child had not been crying. She immediately realized what had happened. The shock and pain of having lost her baby brought forth her most selfish tendencies. It was as if her cruelest instincts bubbled to the surface in one great rush. Her hard life had taught her to think fast in the midst of a crisis and so she instantly hit upon a plan. Quickly, before her companion would awake and know what happened, she exchanged her dead child for the living one of her housemate. When the latter arose, she saw that the infant was dead and, supposing him to be her own, she began to weep uncontrollably. She gently took the tiny, motionless body of the baby in her arms and began to tenderly kiss it. The tears flowed freely down the face of this woman who had so frequently been told that she was loved by those who would soon leave her. Yet this little child, whom she truly loved, had been hers for such a short time. For the first time she had loved someone else with all her heart and now he was gone.

As the woman cradled the infant in her arms, she noticed that the baby didn't have a tiny, violet-colored birthmark above his right eye. Suddenly a horrible suspicion crossed her mind. She glanced warily at her "work companion," who told her not to worry, that she would have another child.

The mother who had been deceived drew close and looked at the baby whom her "friend" clutched tightly in her arms. The latter hurriedly covered the child's face with her shawl—but it was too late. The true mother shouted with the pain and fury of an antelope who feels the sharp teeth of a leopard sinking into his flanks. She knew that she had been robbed of her son. In vain she shouted, fought, and argued, but the thief wouldn't even permit her to touch the child. Desperate, the mother rushed outside and sought help from the authorities.

Solomon's Judgment

The two women were brought before the magistrate. Each earnestly and passionately asserted the living child was hers. No witnesses were available upon whom the judge could call, so he was befuddled and referred the case to a higher court. Once more the two women vociferously presented their arguments to a more experienced, white-haired judge, who listened thoughtfully but ultimately was baffled as well. At last, the case was brought before the supreme tribunal of the land, King Solomon.

As word of the difficult case spread, numerous court ministers and counselors had come to Jerusalem to see what the king would do. The monarch has heard both sides and has ordered that the body of the living child be divided equally between the two women. The executioner awaits only a nod from the king to follow through with his gruesome act.

The woman who had stolen the child cries out, "I want my part! Give me my part!" Her voice is strong and shrill; her eyes, cruel and hateful.

The true mother has no more tears left to cry. Her eyes express deep hurt, but she shows tenderness. She touches the baby's tiny foot once more, looks at the king, and says, "*O my lord, give her the living child, and by no means kill him!*" (1 Kgs. 3:26). To the surprise of all, the other woman angrily demands, "Let him be neither mine nor yours, but divide him."

When Solomon hears the words of the true mother, he immediately halts the execution. The king then rises, looks at the astonished executioner, and proclaims in a loud voice, "*Give the first woman the living child, and by no means kill him; she is his mother*" (1 Kgs. 3:27).

With relief the executioner exhales and quickly sheathes his sword. The mother eagerly wraps her arms around her baby and covers him with kisses. She returns home through the crowded streets of the city and, with the joy of the prodigal son's father, say, *"This my son was dead and is alive again"* (Luke 15:24).

Sunset of a Hero

Royal Wedding

Flaming torches provide abundant, radiant light. Enormous banners are hung from the walls of the hallways and the spacious areas of the royal residence. The day has arrived on which King Solomon is to wed the daughter of the Pharaoh of Egypt (1 Kgs 3:1).

The resonant sounds of the trumpets announce the appearance of the princess. She walks with graceful dignity for she has learned such manners since her early childhood in the Egyptian palace. Jewels and precious stones mounted in pure gold highlight the beauty of her dark skin. She is accompanied by a beautifully arrayed entourage of bridesmaids. On either side of the bridal party, soldiers raise golden-tipped lances from which banners display the colors of the kingdom.

The future husband is dressed in majestic robes. He appears much older than she and is more than her equal in magnificently displaying the customs of the royal court. In all, the wedding is celebrated with the greatest of pomp. The highest dignitaries of the empire of the Nile are present, while the high priest presides over the ceremony in representation of Israel.

Marriage Mismatches

Years pass. The first lady has lost much of her attractiveness. Although the monarch has built a magnificent palace for her with every comfort imaginable, he seldom visits her or even sees her. In fact, King Solomon soon has a large retinue of beautiful wives, all the result of marriages of political expediency made with nearby nations. There is a "Miss Moab," a

Solomon: The Wise and Foolish King

"Miss Ammon," a "Miss Edom," a "Miss Sidon"—a seemingly endless list of wives.

"Your Majesty," inquires the daughter of Pharaoh, "would you be offended if I constructed a small altar to my gods? For too long I have been negligent in worship. All that I request is a small temple and I will be content."

The queen is insistent, and Solomon finally acquiesces. "Very well, you may have your temple. Only it must be small and it must be located in a place that is completely secluded."

"Of course!" the pagan queen responds with a revealing smile.

Sometime later, the daughter of the Ammonite king brings him her own petition. "Your Highness, you have conceded to the request of the daughter of Pharaoh. I also am your wife. Grant me permission to have an altar to *my* gods."

The process is repeated time after time and soon statues of pagan gods dot the city of Jerusalem. Each wife has an altar built on a grander scale than those of the previous wives. In addition, they are no longer positioned in hidden, out-of-the-way locations but rather are displayed in prominent opulence. In time, the inconceivable happens. Solomon himself has begun to worship at the altar of Ashtoreth, the goddess of the Sidonians, and Milcom, the abominable idol of the Ammonites (1 Kings 11:5). Later Solomon builds a high place for Chemosh, the abomination of the Moabites and to Molech, the detestable idol of the children of Ammon (1 Kgs. 11:7).

Cold Comfort

More years go by. The days of Solomon's former glory—the temple of the Lord, the royal palace, the visit of the Queen of Sheba—are all now in the past. The king has just celebrated his fifty-ninth birthday with a grand party, yet somehow to him it seemed horribly melancholic.

The chilly nights of winter seem interminable. The wind and cold penetrate every crack of the palace walls. Vainly the servants try to keep the fireplaces stoked sufficiently to heat the huge rooms. The king lies down to rest in his deeply cushioned bed. He has grown plump over the years and his countenance is now heavily creased. As he lies on a soft bed, tucked under thick blankets, his mind turns back to the events of his life.

He remembers when the Lord first spoke to him, a moment just as fresh as if it had occurred a few moments ago. He was young, just recently crowned king, and was going to Gibeon to offer sacrifices. In those days he loved the Lord and walked in the statutes of his father David (1 Kgs. 3:3), a time when he followed in the ways of *"his first love"* (Rev. 2:4).

On one eventful night, Solomon was deep asleep when he heard a voice. In his dream he realized that the Lord Himself was speaking to him: *"Ask! What shall I give you?"* Solomon responded, *"give to Your servant an understanding heart to judge Your people, that I may discern between good and evil. For who is able to judge this great people of Yours?"* (1 Kgs. 3:5, 9).

He would never forget the Lord's answer. *"Behold, I have done according to your words; see, I have given you a wise and understanding heart, so that there has not been anyone like you before you, nor shall any like you arise after you. And I have also given you what you have not asked: both riches and honour, so that there shall not be anyone like you among the kings all your days."* After a brief pause came the condition, *"So if you walk in My ways, to keep My statutes and My commandments, as your father David walked, then I will lengthen your days"* (1 Kgs. 3:12-14).

After the lavish and God-honouring dedication of the temple, God once again appears to Solomon. *"I have consecrated this house which you have built to put My name there forever, and My eyes and My heart will be there perpetually."* This promise also concludes with a solemn warning: *"But if you or your sons at all turn from following Me, and do not keep My commandments and My statutes which I have set before you, but go and serve other gods and worship them, then I will cut off Israel from the land which I have given them; and this house which I have consecrated for My name I will cast out of My sight"* (1 Kgs. 9:3, 6-7).

The king's heart pounds. The Lord said that he would hold him responsible not only for himself but for all the people of Israel.

Solomon: The Wise and Foolish King

The chilly blast of the winds continues howling, seeping through even the tiniest cracks in the walls. The torches illuminating the palace hallways and chambers nearly flicker out under the brunt of the strong gusts but somehow maintain a tenuous, straining light. Yet in the sumptuous bed of the royal chamber the flame of the king's life has been extinguished.

The Bible Back-Story

Establishing Justice

A narrative such as that of Solomon and the two mothers, in which the wisdom of the individual is lauded, is common in the Middle East. Grotius records such a case: "There is a certain similarity in the account of Ariopharnis, King of the Tracians, who, when three persons claimed to be the sons of the king of the Cimmerii, decided that he was the son who would not obey the command to cast javelins at his father's corpse. The account is given by Diodorus Siculus.[1]

Three thousand years ago, even those members of society who had immoral lives had rights to justice. This right extended to petitioning the audience of the highest dignitaries of the judicial system. Solomon sought to establish justice in his kingdom; indeed, he outlined significant issues in the Book of Proverbs:

- repercussions on the national level, *"Righteousness exalts a nation"* (14:34);
- difficulties in doing justice, *"A disreputable witness scorns justice"* (19:28);
- importance of doing justice, *"To do righteousness and justice is more acceptable to the LORD than sacrifice"* (21:3);
- spiritual reward, *"It is a joy for the just to do justice"* (21:15);
- the danger of favoritism, *"It is not good to show partiality in judgment"* (24:23); and
- political stability as a result, *"The king establishes the land by justice"* (29:4).

Too Much of a Good Thing?

In spite of the fact that Solomon had accumulated vast wealth, he continually sought more. What's more, the people suffered under the burden of heavy taxes. Great architectural achievements, which undoubtedly astounded foreign visitors, offered little consolation to those who bore the brunt of the cost. Little wonder that soon after Solomon died, the ten tribes of the north declared their independence. They must have viewed Jerusalem as a sinkhole of consumption for the wealth produced in other parts of the land.

The Scriptures describe the vastness of Solomon's riches (1 Kgs. 10:14-29). For example, Solomon received 666 talents of gold annually. Given that one talent weighs approximately seventy-seven pounds, he was given almost twenty-six tons a year! God, however, had specifically commanded that the kings of Israel accumulate neither horses, nor wives, nor gold, nor silver (Deut. 17:16-17)—the very things Solomon sought with earnestness.

Particularly shocking is the number of wives that Solomon had: seven hundred (not counting concubines). Imagine their loneliness. If all were treated equally, each wife would spend a single day with the king every two years. Obviously, the encouragement given by the apostle Paul, that husbands love their wives (Eph. 5:25), would have been impossible to follow under such circumstances. The young woman who dreamed of marrying the king and having a happy family life would never have that for which she longed. On the contrary, such a life would be almost like slavery.

Read the Book of Ecclesiastes and feel the burden and gloom of a soul that has known emotional emptiness. It would seem that Solomon was speaking of himself when he wrote, *"Remember now your Creator in the days of your youth, before the difficult days come, and the years draw near when you say, 'I have no pleasure in them'"* (Eccl. 12:1). He had painfully suffered through these very experiences.

Solomon: The Wise and Foolish King

The Biblical Record

Several salient points may be noted concerning the decline of Solomon:

- Clearly, the Lord disapproved of his marriage to the daughter of Pharaoh, as to any unbeliever (Ezra 10:10; 2 Cor. 6:14). We are never even told her name, and she is not referred to as the principal wife of Solomon but always as the daughter of Pharaoh.

- God had promised to prolong Solomon's life if he were obedient (1 Kgs. 3:14; Deut. 17:20). Solomon died at the age of fifty-nine, whereas the biblical standard is seventy years (Ps. 90:10).

- Solomon is not listed among the heroes of the faith in Hebrews 11.

- Jesus mentions Solomon's glories and wisdom (Matt. 6:29; 12:42), but the king is never referenced as an example to follow.

- The biblical account of David ends with a listing of his valiant men (2 Sam. 23:18-39). In contrast, the story of Solomon concludes with a list of the enemies which God has raised up against him (1 Kgs. 11:26-40).

The Struggles in Our Lives

Psychological Logic

An initial reading of 1 Kings 3:17-22 leaves doubt as to who is the true mother. The woman who details the events (whom we will identify as the "first" woman) could be regarded equally well as either the true progenitor of the child or the spurious woman. Upon closer analysis, however, we notice certain indicators of guilt.

For example, the first mother argues her position in a protracted discourse of 140 words (NKJV), while the second woman responds in but 15 words. Additionally, the first refers to the second in a contemptuous manner, tartly calling her "this woman" (1 Kgs. 3:17, 19) instead of "friend" or even "house-mate." The first woman flatteringly employs terms of respect and decorum, addressing the king as "my lord" (1 Kgs. 3:17) and referring to herself as "your maidservant" (1 Kgs. 3:20). The second woman, burdened by the depth of pain in her heart, does not use any elaborate protocol in presenting her case to Solomon. Moreover, the very abundance of specifics that she offers each time she relates the story makes us suspicious the first woman may be the liar. She has thought out her story so well that one is led to disbelieve the account because of the sheer quantity of details. In verses 19-21 we find additional reasons to discount the first woman's story. If, as she claimed, she (the first woman) had been asleep, how could she know that the second woman had rolled over on her child? For the same reason, how could the first woman know the hour at which the second woman arose?

Nearly three thousand years have passed since Solomon employed skillful psychological maneuvering to reveal the true identity of the mother. Modern technology has given us the polygraph machine, better known as a lie detector, an instrument that registers the changes in various biological functions (arterial pressure, pulse, respiration, skin conductivity). This instrument is often able to indicate when an individual makes a false statement. Although Solomon's court lacked modern technology, the wise king was able to cleverly employ an executioner's sword to act as an infallible "lie detector."

Matthew Henry relates, "In order to find the true mother, he couldn't attempt to find whom the baby loved more. Therefore he tried to find who it was who loved the baby more. The two feigned affection for the child but their sincerity was proven when the child was in danger."[2]

In moments of desperation and crisis, we human beings can act in unforeseeable ways. The "false mother" reacted strongly when confronted by the loss of her infant. First, she wanted to have a living child so she stole the other's baby. Second, when she realizes that her subterfuge had been discovered, she quickly demands that the other child die as well—transformed from someone who desperately wanted a living son to someone who is willing, even anxious, to see the surviving child pitilessly killed. The pseudo-mother's attitude is common even today: "If I have to suffer, I want others to suffer too."

We are not told what became of the lying woman. For the rest of her life she would bear the sad burden of the accidental death of her son. Additionally, the entire city would know her as a cruel woman and as a liar which is no small thing because to deliberately give false testimony was a serious crime (Prov. 19:5, 9).

This account, which is graphic and almost brutal, ends happily and with a victory for justice. Love and truth triumph over selfishness and lies. The true mother, whose life and longings had led her into the sad occupation of prostitution, was found to possess pure and profound love. When the years had passed and the baby had grown into a mature man, he could say, "I was a trophy of compassion and love because the king who reigns over Israel is truly wise."

The promise of the Lord to Solomon has been fulfilled: *"See, I have given you a wise and understanding heart, so that there has not been anyone like you before you, nor shall any like you arise after you"* (1 Kgs. 3:12). All these millennia later, God is still fulfilling his promises to his children, whether or not they are royalty.

Losing His Way

How can it be possible that such a wise man, a man who had heard the very voice of God, would later depart from the Lord and embrace idolatry? The question is not only troubling but also a warning to every Christian.

We do not know exactly when Solomon fell into decline. One would suppose that it was a gradual process. All his riches and all his power had been slowly converted into a steadily corrupting influence in his heart. Power and riches in themselves, however, did not corrupt Solomon's faith; the cause was his pursuing after worldly desires. During the reign of Solomon, Jerusalem was not only a strategic commercial junction and a key point in commerce; it was also a cultural center. To bolster that position Solomon contracted marriage with important political allies such as Egypt, Tyre, and other nearby nations. Through the influence of his wives, Solomon was drawn into paganism. He did not heed the scriptural principle later uttered by Jeremiah, *"Let them return to you, But you must not return to them"* (Jer. 15:19b). Solomon thought that he could control the actions of his wives but they ended up controlling his soul (1 Cor. 6:18).

These women showed greater fervor in propagating their false religions than Solomon did in giving testimony of the great Creator God to them. The Lord is angry with the man to whom He has twice revealed Himself (1 Kgs. 11:9). In Solomon's life we find a stern biblical warning fulfilled: *"My brethren, let not many of you become teachers, knowing that we shall receive a stricter judgment"* (Jas. 3:1).

The fact that Solomon had two extraordinary visions of God did not save him from falling into idolatry. We do well to remember that even remarkable spiritual experiences do not confer immunity to temptation and sin.

Solomon's Legacy

Some have suggested that at the end of his days Solomon repented of his departure from the Lord. The fact that the idolatrous high places that he erected remained for nearly three hundred years (until King Josiah finally removed them) seems to belie this idea (2 Kgs. 23:13).

Why would a person who finished his life's journey in such a tragic manner be chosen to write three of the books of Scripture? God graciously uses this man as both a warning and an example to us all. What better individual to choose to write of the vanities of life (Ecclesiastes) than the one who experienced them? As for Proverbs and Song of Solomon, we may well assume that Solomon penned these literary works prior to his tragic departure from the Lord.

Regrettably, the one who wrote the Proverbs, a book so replete with wise teaching, did not follow his own advice. The Book of the Song of Solomon is a literary jewel. I believe it primarily expresses the love of God toward the nation of Israel and, by extension, the love of Christ for the church. As for Solomon himself, he had seven hundred wives and three hundred concubines; other than as an example to avoid, he cannot teach us much about faithfulness and fidelity to a single wife.

Of the temple and the palace of Solomon, nothing remains. His great legacy consists of three books included in the sacred canon. In the sunset of his life, his kingdom, which had spread so extensively and possessed innumerable riches and great military prowess, would be gradually weakened to the point that, shortly after his death, it would be but a shadow of its former glory.

Using Our Gifts

Solomon had profound insight into the practical aspects of psychology. Even before the true mother implored that the child be given to the other woman, he had surely seen compassion in her face and realized she was speaking the truth. Nevertheless the command to divide the baby was given in order that no doubt remained about who was the true mother and who was the impostor. The leader must not only be convinced but also be able to present forceful reasons to others. In addition, Solomon's public display of wisdom would doubtlessly deter his enemies from future confrontations.

I will never have the wisdom of Solomon; no one will ever possess the understanding and knowledge required for every situation. The Christian however, possesses the ultimate resource of the indwelling Holy Spirit. As well, the Lord has promised, *"If any of you lacks wisdom, let him ask of God, who gives to all liberally and without reproach, and it will be given to him"* (Jas. 1:5).

In contrast, deviating from the paths of the Lord will hinder the leader from properly executing judgment. Most likely, justice and wisdom accompanied Solomon only during those years when he followed the commandments of the Lord. Toward the end of his life, the situation seemed to have changed. His only child, Prince Rehoboam, declared he had placed a heavy yoke on the people and chastised them with whips (1 Kgs. 12:11). It's improbable that he could act this way and, at the same time, remain a just and righteous king.

Solomon did not teach his son how to properly govern the people. Without this transference of leadership qualities, the nation soon dissolved. In fact, there seems to have been little attempt to develop leadership abilities in any of his associates. Benaniah, Solomon's general, is occasionally mentioned, but only as the one who executes Solomon's enemies. The High Priest is mentioned only in passing. One has the impression that Solomon was a natural leader but also lived in isolation. David had the prophet Nathan to advise and admonish him, but Solomon had no one.

Comparison, Contrast and Ideas to Expand

Solomon	The "Greater than Solomon"
The son of a king	The Son of God
His riches disappeared	His riches are forever
His servants were his for a time	His servants serve Him eternally
His wisdom did not keep him from falling	He never fell or failed. He was Holy.
He had a transitory earthly reign	He has a eternal heavenly reign
He could never enter the Most Holy Place	He entered the Most Holy Place (Heb 9:24)

Weapons that would never fulfil their purpose

- Abraham's knife (Gen 22:10).
- Solomon's sword of justice (1 Kings 3:24).
- Herod's sword drawn to execute Peter (Acts 12:2,3).
- The jailer's sword which he had planned suicide (Acts 16:27).

Solomon: The Wise and Foolish King

A weapon that did fulfil its purpose

> "Awake, O sword, against My Shepherd,
> Against the Man who is My Companion,"
> Says the Lord of hosts.
> "Strike the Shepherd...
>
> Zechariah 13:7

A Comparison with John 8; similarities and contrasts

Many have drawn parallels between the story of Solomon's judgment for the true mother (1 Kgs. 3:16-28) and Jesus' encounter with a woman (John 8):

1 Kings Woman	John 8 Woman
The mother was a harlot	The woman was an adulterer.
She is brought before Solomon	She is brought before Jesus.
She is judged	She is judged.
She was in danger of losing her son	She was in danger of losing her life.
The situation is resolved by a command	The situation is resolved by a question.
Solomon administers justice	Jesus grants forgiveness.
The result is life and joy	The result is life and joy.

Solomon's Prayer	Scriptural Promises
Cases that are difficult to determine (v. 22).	If any of you lacks wisdom (Jas. 1:5).
Military (or spiritual) defeat (v. 24).	We are more than conquerors (Rom. 8:37).
Drought (v. 26)	Out of his heart will flow rivers of living water (John 7:38).
Famine (v. 28)	He who comes to Me shall never hunger (John 6:35).

Our Struggle with Good & Evil

Solomon's Prayer	Scriptural Promises
Disease (v. 28)	Confess your trespasses... that you may be healed (Jas. 5:16).
Exile (v. 38)	Beloved...as sojourners and pilgrims (1 Pet. 2:11).

Discussion Starters

1. In both accounts from Solomon's life, what do we learn about lies and their consequences?

2. For all his wisdom, what dangers of incorporating pagan practices did Solomon ignore?

3. Describe a modern-day tragedy of one who begins well but does not finish well.

4. How does God speaks to His children today?

Part 2

FOLLOWING FATHER'S FOOTSTEPS

Chapter 6

ASA: HIGHS AND LOWS

"Important news! Queen Maacah has abdicated!" The announcement spreads like wildfire through the streets of Jerusalem.

The Magnitude-8 Earthquake

Enough Is Enough!

"It can't be true!" says a man who had been walking quickly but stopped short when he heard the shocking report.

"Are you telling me she resigned?" a woman asks the street vendor who gave her the news.

If the streets were abuzz with rumors, the palace was truly bustling with excitement. In the hallways the servants' whispers are hushed but excited: "Did *she* resign or did they 'resign *for* her'?"

The story began a few weeks earlier, when the highest religious authorities arrived at the royal palace to speak with the king. "Majesty, we are most thankful to the Lord for the dedication to God that you have so clearly demonstrated all these years. In addition we are very pleased with your decision to remove the altars of pagan worship, the high places, and the groves and stone altars of Asherah. We know that

God blesses those who honour Him and the Lord has blessed you very richly."

The king expresses his appreciation with a nod of his head. Nevertheless he can see the visitors have something more to say. "That is very good. But I do not imagine that this is all you have to tell me."

The eldest of the assembled men steps forward. His white hair reveals his many years, years of steadfastly serving God. His face shows the determination and firmness resulting from a lifetime of faith and trust in the Omnipotent God. "Your Majesty, with all due respect and with gratitude for your faithfulness to God, we nevertheless must say that we are concerned about the example being set by your grandmother, the Queen Mother."

His words are met with silence. The king's face turns pale. Nearby are seated the royal counselors and ministers; the king glances toward them, but they look perplexed and say nothing.

The old priest continues, "My King, you destroy the altars of Asherah and the high places but the Queen Mother rebuilds and restores them."

A prince asks for a word. "The Queen Mother has always persisted in this wicked practice. Everyone knows she isn't going to change. She says that she isn't doing any harm, that we should be more open to other ways of worship, and that we should not be so judgmental. She states furthermore that it is our duty to humbly submit to her, the Queen Mother."

The king clearly struggles with this difficult decision. At length he stands and says to those assembled, "I command that Queen Mother Maacah renounce her position."

Sounds of approval erupt immediately in the spacious throne room. "Long live King Asa!" someone shouts and the others take up the chant. "Long live King Asa!"

"We Rest on You"

Before the king's historic declaration, something very unusual had occurred. The kingdom was at peace, prosperous, and stable. The king had convened his ministers and told them,

Asa: Highs and Lows

"Let us rebuild these cities and make walls around them, and towers, gates, and bars...because we have sought the LORD our God; we have sought Him, and He has given us rest on every side" (2 Chron. 14:7).

At the time, no one suspected that this was simply the calm before the storm. King Asa had been diligent in cleansing the nation of Judah of pagan idols and high places dedicated to false worship. All seemed to be going well, but then distressing news arrived. Zerah the Ethiopian had come to war against Judah with an army of one million men, reinforced by one hundred thousand cavalry troops (Josephus) and three hundred chariots.

King Asa quickly assembled his own men and marched out to defend the homeland. His army had scarcely half the troops of the enemy—three hundred thousand men of Judah who carried shields and spears and two hundred and eighty thousand men of Benjamin (2 Chron. 14:8). Hurriedly the troops commanded by Asa rushed to meet them and took up their positions before the Judean town of Mareshah. There the two enemy armies prepared for battle.

From the Ethiopian camp, sounds of a great religious ritual dedicated to the gods pierced the air. Musical instruments resonated with mournful, satanic notes.

King Asa, in contrast, gathered the men for a simple but resolute prayer: *"LORD, it is nothing for You to help, whether with many or with those who have no power; help us, O LORD our God, for we rest on You, and in Your Name we go against this multitude. O LORD, You are our God; do not let man prevail against you!"* (2 Chron. 14:11). The king was filled with a sense of profound peace; he knew that the LORD was with them.

At the moment the Judean army moved forward—as King Asa shouted, "Attack!"—something happened. The Ethiopian soldiers were firmly in position and confident of the battle's outcome when suddenly chaos broke out within their ranks. Some of the squadrons rushed backwards; others dashed to the outer flanks of the battlefront. Chariots careened into each other. Horses reared up and galloped wildly through the confused troops. Men were knocked down and trampled. Commanders shouted contradictory orders. It was as if a meteor had fallen into the midst of the camp. *"So the LORD struck the Ethiopians before Asa and Judah, and the Ethiopians fled"* (2 Chron. 14:12).

At King Asa's command, the Judean soldiers rushed to pursue the fleeing and disoriented enemy. The Ethiopians vainly tried to escape, but one by one they fell before the swords of Asa's men, *"for they were broken before the LORD and His army. And they carried away very much spoil"* (2 Chron. 14:13b).

The Reign of Asa

A Prophet Speaks

Soon after the victory over the Ethiopians, God sent a message to Asa through a prophet, Azariah the son of Oded.

The prophet speaks purposefully, *"Hear me, Asa, and all Judah and Benjamin. The LORD is with you while you are with Him. If you seek Him, He will be found by you; but if you forsake Him, He will forsake you. For a long time Israel has been without the true God, without a teaching priest and, without law;"* (2 Chron. 15:2-3).

The king listens attentively and respectfully. Azariah finishes the divine injunction by saying, *"But you, be strong and do not let your hands be weak, for your work shall be rewarded!"* (2 Chron. 15:7).

Although Asa had sought to cleanse Judah of idolatry, there was still much to do. The king immediately *"took courage and removed the abominable idols from all the land of Judah and Benjamin…and he restored the altar of the LORD that was before the vestibule of the LORD"* (2 Chron. 15:8). Afterwards Asa made a pact along with all the people of Judah, promising to seek after the Lord with all their heart and strength. The people responded with joy and enthusiasm, with shouting, trumpets, and rams' horns (2 Chron. 15:14).

This celebration of dedication and the recent military victory over the Ethiopians represent the highest points in the public life of King Asa. The Bible confirms the peace that pervaded the land after the people had *"sworn with all their heart."*

Asa: Highs and Lows

The Lord was *"found by them, and the LORD gave them rest all around"* (2 Chron. 15:15).

The Test of Time

Twenty-one years have now passed since the great celebration of consecration to the Lord. During those years the neighboring nation of Israel, under the rule of wicked King Baasha, has begun a tremendous military build-up. King Asa of Judah has gradually grown spiritually cold and detached. The great revival is now little more than a distant memory.

One day Asa convenes the military rulers and all civil and religious authorities. The spacious palace hall is replete with luxurious fixtures. The dignitaries and distinguished men wait patiently until at last the monarch is announced with great pomp. He addresses them, "Sirs, we are confronted by a grave and critical situation. Our enemy, King Baasha of Israel, has come up against us with an enormous army. Just four and a half miles from here, he is rebuilding Ramah with the intention to besiege Jerusalem. This blockade of our city is not yet complete, but we have no idea how much longer we have until we are totally encircled. I wish to know what the generals think."

One of the officers rises and says, "Your Majesty, it is true that the enemy has a much larger army than ours and that he enjoys abundant provisions. We are already rationing our supplies. If the present state of affairs continues we will inevitably exhaust our food and water resources. I propose we mount a raid and attack the enemy with all available forces. We should seek the blessing of God. We know that we will incur losses but if we are not successful the kingdom is lost. Your Excellency knows very well the cruelty of Baasha and his generals."

Other military officers suggest simple variations of the proffered plan. One general rises and speaks, "Your Highness, to attack Baasha in our present state of strength and with the enemy commanding well-prepared defenses is impossible. I believe the only solution is to attack simultaneously with a frontal assault as well as mounting a maximum effort attack against the rear of the enemy's forces accompanied by a flanking maneuver."

With a mocking smile another officer asks, "How can we simultaneously attack from behind and charge the enemy from the front if we can barely muster sufficient forces to even leave the city?"

"It's very simple," responds the general, "we only have to ask for foreign help. I know that King Ben-Hadad of Syria is quite willing to help us...if we pay him enough."

The king wonders, *But where could we find sufficient money? The royal treasuries are nearly exhausted.* With great difficulty he struggles to stand up. He is no longer the confident ruler of twenty years before, the one who showed such great trust in the Lord when confronted by a superior enemy. With a trembling voice he says, "I am willing to surrender all my personal treasures. But we will need to send the Syrians treasures from the Lord's temple as well."

The High Priest rises at once. With no attempt to disguise his deep anxiety he says, "Your Majesty, is there nothing we can do to avoid touching the temple treasures? They are not ours. They belong to the Lord!"

In a voice of exhausted surrender the ruler responds, "There is nothing else to do. The Syrian king will require all that we have. We have no other option but to use the gold and silver from the temple."

Syria Answers

When a messenger from Syria arrives in Jerusalem, he delivers a sealed document. "My esteemed friend and honourable King Asa," begins the message. "With much pleasure I accept your proposal along with the details that were previously stipulated. I have therefore ordered my generals to proceed with plans for an incursion into the territory of the nation of Israel." It is signed by Ben-Hadad, king of Syria.

Later, as the Syrian armies approach the borders of Israel, Baasha the king of Israel immediately abandons preparations for an attack on Jerusalem and instead hastily prepares a defense of his own territory. When news of the Baasha's abrupt change

Asa: Highs and Lows

in plans reaches Jerusalem, there is great rejoicing. Hordes of people gather together and shout, "Long live King Asa! Long live our liberator!" In the days and weeks following the Israelite withdrawal, a steady stream of Jews travel to Ramah to tear down the siege structures that King Baasha had been preparing. The people use those same stones and materials to fortify the towns of Geba and Mizpah (2 Chron. 16:6).

Although the citizens of Jerusalem continue to pour out praise to King Asa for having saved their nation from the enemy without even having shed a drop of blood, the elders and priests are not so happy. They know a huge price has been paid.

The monarch has a great feast to celebrate the "victory." The ministers, generals, and officers of the court gather in the great hall of the palace to commemorate their diplomatic achievement. The next day the ruler gets out of bed with a terrible headache, the consequence of excessive libations of the previous night. He slowly dresses and reluctantly prepares himself for the day. Stepping into the main hall of the palace he is approached by a servant.

"Your Highness, the seer Hanani has arrived and desires an audience with you."

"Inform him that I am not well. I will see him tomorrow."

The servant withdraws but rather quickly returns. "My King, he insists and says that he has an urgent message from the Lord." The king nods reluctantly.

Hanani enters the hall solemnly. He is some seventy years old and his hair and beard have grown gray with age, but his eyes reveal great strength of spirit and resolve.

"Because you have relied on the king of Syria," Hanani begins, *"and have not relied on the LORD your God, therefore the army of the king of Syria has escaped from your hand. Were the Ethiopians and the Lubim not a huge army with very many chariots and horsemen? Yet, because you relied on the LORD, He delivered them into your hand."*

The face of Asa has grown ashen. The seer proceeds with his words of reprimand and chastisement: *"For the eyes of the LORD run to and fro throughout the whole earth, to show Himself strong on behalf of those whose heart is loyal to Him"* (2 Chron. 16:7-9).

Sickness of Soul and Soles

The king has become angry, his face flushed. "You! Who do you think you are to speak to me in this manner? I am the king! Never in my life has anyone spoken to me with such insolence. I have been an example of steadfastness to the Lord. I cleansed the land of idols and destroyed the places of foreign worship. I broke down the high places. I…I…"

Hanani raises his hand and then points to the king. *"You have done foolishly; therefore from now on you shall have wars"* (2 Chron. 16:9).

The king is enraged and orders, "Take him to the prison! He is guilty of disrespect and telling falsehoods. Lock him in the darkest cell of the dungeon and give him only bread and water."

Hanani is led brusquely out of the palace. King Asa leaves by a side door and walks out to the royal gardens. He takes a few steps and then feels a sudden cramp in the calf muscles of his leg. He stops to rub it. After just a few more paces, he feels painful muscle contractions in both legs.

Meanwhile Hanani has been thrust into the dungeon, into a chamber so small that there is no room to walk. Nevertheless, he has no regrets as he settles down in the damp quarters. Hanani raises his voice in a song of praise to the Lord, as have so many other faithful servants of God through the centuries (Acts 16:25).

The next morning the king convenes his ministers and declares, "I decree that whoever criticizes or makes a negative comment with respect to anything I have done will be immediately arrested and jailed." The Bible records that *"Asa oppressed some of the people at that time"* (2 Chron. 16:10b).

In the next several months the king has increasing difficulty in walking. The royal courtesans realize that the problem is growing serious and say, "Your Majesty, with all respect, we believe that you must do something soon about the problem with your legs."

Asa: Highs and Lows

"It's nothing serious. I'm sure it will pass."

The condition only grows worse until finally King Asa is struck with extreme and debilitating pain after but a few steps. He orders his servants, "Hurry, bring the finest physicians that can be found in the kingdom. Send to Egypt if necessary. I want the best!"

One of the oldest of the king's servants whispers to another, "Why doesn't the king seek the Lord? As the psalmist wrote, *He is the one who heals all our diseases.*"

The king's condition continues to deteriorate. He is forced to hang his legs out over the side of the bed to find even the slightest relief. His toes have begun to darken in color as the blood flow to them diminishes. King Asa has been treated by the best Egyptian physicians, who have tried several remedies and applied many ointments, but his health only worsens. The ruler's feet are ice cold and stiff as marble. The intense pain is nearly unbearable, even at rest.

A few weeks later the mournful sound of trumpets and flutes is heard in the streets of Jerusalem. The king has died. *"They buried him in his own tomb, which he had made for himself in the City of David; and they laid him in the bed which was filled with spices and various ingredients prepared in a mixture of ointments. They made a very great burning for him"* (2 Chron. 16:14).

The Bible Back-Story

Power and Possessions

A glimpse of the military and political power wielded by the generals of the army is clearly indicated by the mention of their names along with their respective armies (2 Chron. 17:14, 18). In each case these generals commanded more than one hundred thousand men.

The Ethiopians were most likely mercenary soldiers who were in the service of Egypt. Certainly it would be unlikely that Egypt would permit that an enemy army pass through its territory. The army was probably composed of either Nubian or Cushite soldiers.[1]

According to the historical account recorded in 2 Chronicles, the deposing of Queen Maachah took place following the Ethiopian invasion. Her removal came during the revival that followed the call to repentance preached by Azariah the prophet.

At the time of the great celebration in the capital, held in the fifteenth year of Asa's reign, there were seven hundred cattle and seven thousand sheep which were offered in sacrifice.

Medical Notes

It is unlikely that King Asa suffered from gout, as is the contention of many commentators. Gout does not result in death. Rather Asa most likely suffered from a disease which, unfortunately, is by no means rare. Probably he had what is known as peripheral arterial disease, or arteriosclerosis, of the lower extremities. Just as the drains in house plumbing may clog due to grease or other obstructions, arteriosclerosis of the arteries in the legs and feet results from blockages due to cholesterol and other materials.

The clinical evolution of the disease can be predicted with a great deal of precision. If there is no surgical intervention using a bypass or angioplasty (obviously unavailable in the days of Asa), gangrene of the toes sets in. The toes become discolored and black. Eventually the gangrene extends to the foot and gradually to the entire leg. The phrase *"his malady was severe"* (2 Chron. 16:12) may also be translated "it extended upwards."[2] When the disease advances to involve the legs, amputation is often the only recourse. The fact that perfumes and ointments were used in the treatment of Asa's condition is exactly what would be expected in the case of gangrene. The odor resulting from necrosis and tissue death is very intense and offensive.

The Egyptian physicians utilized magic arts in their treatments. These practices would include invocations to their gods and supplication for healing.

Asa: Highs and Lows

The Struggles in Our Lives

Rest upon God

At times life seems to amble along in tranquility. The years roll by and all is well. There are no particular job stresses, the family is in good health, the children are growing and doing well in school. But then suddenly something happens and our entire family and social structures seem to collapse, as if a magnitude-8 earthquake has struck. Among the many possible causes are health problems, job loss, and a crisis within the family.

It was during the years in which the kingdom of Judah enjoyed rest that King Asa wisely built walls around the cities and constructed strong defensive fortifications. Likewise it is during those tranquil moments in our lives that we should strengthen ourselves in the Lord through the reading and study of the Bible. By this manner we will be *"strengthened with might through His Spirit in the inner man"* (Eph. 3:16).

Many Christians begin their spiritual lives confronted by overwhelming difficulties and perhaps even failures, but little by little these individuals learn to grow in the Lord and eventually overcome discouragement and defeat. They come to enjoy the peace and happiness of a life resting in Christ. On the other hand, there are those who begin well but who do not finish well. Even the apostle Paul was aware of this possibility when he wrote, *"But I discipline my body and bring it into subjection, lest, when I have preached to others, I myself should become disqualified"* (1 Cor. 9:27).

King Asa's faithfulness and dedication to the Lord are of such a high caliber that he even makes painful decisions involving his own family. Doubtless it was very difficult for him to remove his grandmother from her position. He surely received a great deal of criticism for this action not only from within his family but from without as well. Hundreds of years later, the Lord Jesus would say, *"He who loves father or mother more than Me is not worthy of Me; and he who loves son or daughter more than Me is not worthy of Me"* (Matt. 10:37).

Prior to battle, Asa said a prayer that was a burning supplication (2 Chron. 14:11). The Bible says that he did not so much speak the prayer as cried out to the Lord. In his fervent petition he praises the omnipotence of God, knowing that it is nothing for Him to help, and recognizes that his forces are weak and incapable of confronting such a powerful enemy. After pouring out his heart, Asa shows absolute confidence in God, trusting in His strength: *"Help us, O LORD our God, for we rest on You, and in Your name we go against this multitude"* (2 Chron. 14:11).

In the 1890s Edith G. Cherry was inspired by Asa's prayer to write a poem. A few years later it was set to Jean Sibelius's "Finlandia" and became the beloved hymn "We Rest on Thee."

Listen to God

King Asa had started well in ridding the land of idols and the worship of foreign gods, but there was much left to do. The words of the prophet Azariah were revealing: *"For a long time Israel has been without the true God, without a teaching priest, and without law"* (2 Chron. 15:3). A partial, superficial rinsing of what are abominable in the eyes of the Lord is simply not enough. Paul expresses the Lord's wishes clearly, *"Let us cleanse ourselves from all filthiness of the flesh and spirit, perfecting holiness in the fear of God"* (2 Cor. 7:1).

At times we might wonder at the effectiveness of the preaching of God's Word. In the case of Azariah, the results are evident. In his first appearance he bore the Lord's message immediately after the victory over the Ethiopians. We all can learn from the following chain of events:

1. Prior to the battle, King Asa prays.
2. God answers the king's prayer and gives a resounding victory.
3. The Lord sends a message through the prophet that says, in effect, "you must seek Me and obey Me."
4. At this point, Asa responds positively to God's message and continues to cleanse the land of idols.

Asa: Highs and Lows

5. In the fifteenth year of his reign, King Asa holds a great celebration and the people pledge faithfulness to God.

When we listen to God however He chooses to communicate with us, we stay on the right path.

Do Not Take Forgiveness Lightly

There is a certain manner of thinking often held (perhaps unvoiced) among Christians that in effect gives license to sin. This mistaken philosophy holds that we can do as we please and then, if we will but later say we are sorry and have a modicum of repentance, God will forgive us and all will be well. While this notion is at least partially based on a Bible truth in that God does indeed forgive those who truly repent, it stretches and expands the biblical principle to unbiblical limits and arrives at an erroneous conclusion.

In fact, this way of thinking gives rise to the idea that one can sin repeatedly and remain confident there will be no consequences. It is likely that such an attitude was pervasive in Judah during the latter years of the reign of King Asa. The prophet Azariah had warned, *"If you forsake Him* (God), *He will forsake you"* (2 Chron. 15:2), and his words proved tragically true.

Repent and Return to God

During his later years Asa took his eyes off the Lord. He began to doubt God's ability, and perhaps His willingness, to defeat the enemy. It is also quite possible that a specific sin in Asa's life led him to believe that God would not hear him.

Asa committed several serious errors in seeking help from the king of Syria:

- He showed a lack of trust that the Lord would give them the victory;
- He took the treasures that belonged to the Lord and gave them to a nation that had been an enemy and would continue to be hostile to Judah;
- He formed an "unequal yoke" alliance with an unbelieving king;

111

- He became a bad example to his people by his lack of confidence in the One who had to lead and teach them; and

- He induced the king of Syria to break a pledge.

The aid of the Syrian king was not needed. God is constantly observing our lives; if our hearts are upright, He will strengthen our hands. Hanani clearly declared that with the help of the Lord, Judah could have had the victory against Baasha, King of Israel (2 Chron. 16:9).

Again, when Asa was confronted by a serious illness, he did not seek the help of the Lord. Did he honestly think he was more likely to be healed by the Egyptian physicians? Perhaps he believed that his treatment of Hanani meant God would no longer hear him. One of Asa's descendants, Hezekiah, when finding himself in a similar situation, prayed to God and the Lord responded by prolonging his life. Jeremiah expressed the folly of not seeking the Lord's willing aid with his well-known words: *"Is there no balm in Gilead? Is there no physician there?"* (Jer 8:22). The Lord does not condemn us for going to a physician when we are ill. He Himself said, *"Those who are well have no need of a physician, but those who are sick"* (Mark 2:17). Believers place their confidence not in the physician but in the Lord, who uses the physician as His instrument. They pray and ask God to give their doctors wisdom and skill.

Some well-known commentators suggest that, toward the very end of his life, Asa turned to the Lord once again and sought Him with all his heart.[3] The fact that his son was a good and God-fearing king gives weight to this suggestion. In addition, the great honour shown to Asa in death implies that he was a king much beloved by the people. The body was carefully prepared for burial, with aromatic spices and mixtures of ointments, which indicates that his interment was witnessed by a great multitude. Asa's body was buried in a tomb that he himself had prepared, a detail the Scriptures often use as a sign of divine approval.

When the Judge of all the earth looks the whole of Asa's life, neither the darkness of his lack of faith nor his anger against the servant of God stand out. The divine appraisal of Asa's life was that he *"did what was good and right in the eyes of the Lord his God"* (2 Chron. 14:2). Moreover, only one person in the history of this world has been totally holy, innocent, and pure, and that is Jesus Christ (Heb. 7:26).

Asa passed his final exam, and so can we. In the words of the Apostle Paul, we can rejoice that *"He who has begun a good work in you will complete it until the day of Jesus Christ…forgetting those things which are behind and reaching forward to those things which are ahead, I press toward the goal for the prize of the upward call of God in Christ Jesus"* (Phil. 1: 6b; 3:13-14).

Using Our Gifts

Family and Practical Matters

A leader must have an exemplary testimony with regard to his or her home life. This is by no means always easy because one of Satan's favored tactics is to stain our testimony by means of attacks directed against the family. It is exceedingly important that others recognize that the leader does not show favoritism or partiality to those of his own circle of friends or relatives. At times, doing what is necessary can be very difficult, but King Asa is an example of one who did what was necessary.

The ideal leader is one who possesses the rare combination of being a practical minded person, but at the same time exhibits a deeply spiritual walk with God. That combination was seen in the early years of Asa's reign, in that he took practical steps to strengthen the nation's defenses during an opportune period. When a crisis arose, he sought the Lord's face and rested in His strength.

The leader sees things that are not obvious to others. How was it possible, for example, that nobody noticed or was seriously concerned that the altar in front of the gate was in disrepair? Certainly not because it was hidden from view. Rather, the people had grown accustomed to it and had become careless concerning it.

Our Struggle with Good & Evil

King Asa's leadership during the first fifteen years of his reign was characterized by prayer and obedience to the Lord. Notably, as a result of Asa's promise to seek the Lord, rest and peace came upon all the land (2 Chron. 15).

Guilt by Associations

One of the dangers that confronts every leader is that of forming alliances of convenience with persons or groups with convictions that are different from or even contrary to ours. *"Can two walk together unless they be agreed?"* (Amos 3:3). Every leader must be able to recognize dangerous associations, particularly those which may gradually lead us astray (2 John 9-10). Forming partnerships or coalitions with groups having questionable principles may make it possible to recruit more individuals than before, but without the blessing of God it is all for naught.

The phrase *"let there be a treaty between you and me"* is tragic. Unfortunately, within a few years Asa's own son Jehoshaphat would make the same error and form a military coalition with King Ahab of Israel. As a result Jehoshaphat nearly loses his life (2 Chron. 18:3). In contrast, years later Nehemiah, who had been offered help from his enemies, soundly rejected it (Neh. 6:3).

Maintaining Integrity

How could Asa make such a promising start and yet not finish well? We must not forget that Asa ruled as king for forty-one years. During such a long administration virtually any president or ruler (not to mention we ourselves) would have committed a number of errors. In all this it may be seen that God's warning is still important today: *"Therefore let him who thinks he stands take heed lest he fall"* (1 Cor. 10:12)

In the story of King Asa we see the dangerous situation of leaders who become authoritarian. In time they conclude they are infallible. The one who is wise and mature will listen to the suggestions of brothers and sisters and accept their corrections with humility. A leader who is not accountable to others is like a time bomb placed in a deadly location.

Asa: Highs and Lows

Plundering the gold and silver consecrated to the Lord in order to buy the services of Ben-Hadad can in no way be justified. Even though Asa himself (and his father) had donated the gold to the temple, the overriding principle is this: what has been given to the Lord is no longer ours. Just so, leaders in the church must be very careful with money given for the Lord's purposes, donated at great personal sacrifice. No funds given to God should ever be used for personal reasons.

When Asa ordered the imprisonment of Hanani, he earned the sad distinction of being the first king of Judah to punish a servant of God that way. The prophet is the true spiritual leader of the nation (2 Tim. 2:12) because, from the gloomy prison cell, emanates the brilliant light of God's truth and Hanani's dedication to Him. Meanwhile, the king, seated on his throne and adorned with trinkets of gold, has forfeited his place of spiritual leadership in the nation. In spite of all the exquisitely fashioned oil lamps that beautified the chambers of the palace, the spiritual darkness was palpable.

The hero in this Bible account is Hanani, the seer. Many in Judah recognized his spiritual leadership; consequently, the king tyrannized them. In order to remain as steadfast as Hanani, one must have the characteristics of leadership combined with courage, firm determination, and complete faithfulness to the Lord.

Discussion Starters

1. What should one do when a family member opposes spiritual things? Do you believe Asa was overly zealous or fanatical in deposing his own grandmother?

2. How does this story show us the power of prayer? What were the important elements of King Asa's prayer?

3. What are the specific reasons why it was wrong for Asa to seek help from Beh-Hadad?

4. What are contemporary examples of a person or group starting well and then going astray?

5. In what ways can you help each other consistently do what is "good and right in the eyes of the Lord"?

Chapter 7

JEHOSHAPHAT: ENEMIES AND ALLIES

A military messenger carries a scroll to the king. The communiqué warns that an enormous army is preparing to attack the nation of Judah.

Music Instead of Spears

Enemy Times Three

The forces against King Jehoshaphat, son of Asa, are from three rival kingdoms—Moab, Ammon, and Edom. The army has already encroached on Judean territory and is encamped close to the eastern border, near En Gedi.

Jehoshaphat is surrounded by his commanders and generals who express concern over their lack of military strength. What's more, they say, the enemy is well supplied and well trained (2 Chron. 20:1-2).

With a firm voice the king replies, "My generals and commanders, we are going to seek the Lord. With Him there is strength and if it is His will we shall win. We know that He is able to give us the victory. I hereby proclaim a fast throughout Judah that the Lord may hear us and answer our petition."

Some days later an enormous multitude has gathered around the temple in Jerusalem. People have arrived from every region of Judah; there are not only men but also women and even children (2 Chron. 20:4, 13).

A young child anxiously asks his father, "Why is mommy weeping?"

The father barely holds back his own tears and answers, "Evil men have come against us. They want to kill us. But don't fear, my son, we are trusting in the Lord of Hosts."

"Daddy, what will happen if the Lord doesn't help us?"

The father lifts his eyes toward heaven and says, "The Lord has always helped us in our time of need. He has never failed us."

With the multitude now assembled, King Jehoshaphat raises his arms and prays, "We cry out to You in our affliction, and You will hear and save us. We do not know what to do, but our eyes are upon You."

Jahaziel the Levite stands to bring the Lord's response. Nervously the people await the answer. With a firm voice the prophet declares, "Do not be afraid or dismayed. The battle is not yours, but God's!"

God's Battle Plan

The prophet continues the Lord's message, with detailed instructions. *"Tomorrow go down against them. They will surely come up by the Ascent of Ziz, and you will find them at the end of the brook before the Wilderness of Jeruel. You will not need to fight in this battle"* (2 Chron. 20:16-17).

"What are you telling me?" asks Jehoshaphat. "We won't have to fight?"

"Yes, your Majesty. The Lord has revealed to me that we have only to stand by and see the Lord's victory. Position yourselves, stand still, and see the salvation of the Lord, who is with you!"

"But our army is not yet prepared for battle. We need at least another week to bring it up to strength."

Jehoshaphat: Enemies and Allies

Jahaziel reiterates, *"Tomorrow go out against them, for the LORD is with you"* (2 Chron. 20:17).

The following day the troops leave the city of Jerusalem. They direct themselves to the desert of Tekoa (about four and a half miles to the south of Bethlehem). The battalions of the different cities of Judah are banded together. The men march forth to the sound of trumpets and the applause of thousands and thousands who have gathered to see them off. King Jehoshaphat stands in the gate of the city and encourages them, saying, "Trust in the Lord your God and you will be safe. Believe the prophets and you will do well." As the last of the troops pass through the gate, Jehoshaphat hurries to the front of the column. He will lead the troops himself.

The three enemy armies—comprising many thousands of soldiers prepare themselves for engagement. The army of Moab is deployed on the left flank, on the right flank; is the army of Ammon, and in the center is that of Seir (Edom). The cavalry along with the war chariots initiate the attack. The infantry follow with spears and shields. The horizon is bright with sunlight reflecting off the weapons.

The Sounds of Victory

In front of the attacking enemy forces, the army of Judah is ready. King Jehoshaphat immediately gives the order to advance, but those who go forward are neither the chariots nor the cavalry. The ones in the vanguard have no shields or swords or spears, but rather trumpets and horns and cymbals. At the very head of the troops marches the king, joyful and confident; it's as if he has come to the battlefield simply to celebrate the victory. As the musicians proceed, the rest of the army marches forth behind them, making a noise like that of a thousand rusty trains trying to start up.

Curiously, instead of battle chants, the hearty voices of the soldiers boom forth with songs of praise. The Levites sing, *"Oh, give thanks to the LORD, for He is good! For His mercy endures forever"* (Ps. 136:1). What begins as a refrain sung by the musicians has become an immense chorus. The Levites sing, *"To Him who struck down great kings"*; the soldiers in thunderous response declare, *"For His mercy endures forever"* (Ps. 136:17). As the singing reverberates through the valley, the procession draws near to the hillside of Kish.

Then something unprecedented occurs. The Moabite army that was advancing on the left flank suddenly and inexplicably makes a ninety-degree turn and falls with brutal fury on the forces of Edom. At the same time the Ammonite regiments on the right flank turn left and throw themselves with savage ferocity against their allies in the middle.

Confusion reigns. War chariots race through a battlefield strewn with the dead and dying. Thousands of arrows crisscross the sky. Men fall to rise no more. From a rocky outcrop one can look down on a human whirlwind of soldiers fighting in desperate hand-to-hand combat. Yet on the far side, the army still moves forward. The singers are confidently in front as they intone, *"And rescued us from our enemies, for His mercy endures forever"* (Ps. 136:24). Eventually the only sounds are those of the jubilant musicians and soldiers. Together they shout with joy, *"For His mercy endures forever!"*

As the vultures fly lazily overhead in increasingly tight concentric circles awaiting their opportunity to feast, Jehoshaphat and his men recover a vast amount of plunder. The quantity is so great it takes three days to gather it all. *"On the fourth day they assembled in the Valley of Berachah, for there they blessed the LORD"* (2 Chron. 20:26).

The triumphant caravan returns to Jerusalem. There are no prisoners, *"for the Lord had made them rejoice over their enemies"* (2 Chron. 20:27b).

The Sunken Ships of Jehoshaphat

The Invincible Armada

It was a rather unusual setting for such magnificent and gala ceremony to be celebrated—a shipyard on the southern coast of Judah. An elaborate seating area has been specially constructed near the windblown site. The flags of Israel and of Judah were fluttering in the stiff breeze while military bands filled the air with music and pomp and the feeling of festive gaiety.

Just at this moment, the king of Israel arrives in his chariot and with great ceremony walks toward his seating place. He is dressed in the finest of regal attire. Applause erupts from all those present. The trumpeters herald his arrival with harmonious peals. Next Jehoshaphat, king of Judah, makes his entrance. Again the trumpets sound and the assembled officials and the crowds express their approval with enthusiastic clapping. The two men sit side by side on elegant thrones that have been strategically placed for the ensuing viewing (Ps. 1:1). After they are seated, a single trumpet announces a military parade.

First to march are the troops of Israel, followed by columns of soldiers from Judah strutting proudly past the two kings and the assembled officials. When at last the final troops depart the parade ground, silence falls. Ahaziah, king of Israel, rises to his feet and begins a protracted and rambling discourse the great benefits of a new undertaking. With the launching of a great fleet of ships, jointly sponsored by his own nation and that of Judah, Israel will enjoy increased commerce and trade with foreign nations, particularly Ophir. He speaks of the wealth from the exotic goods soon to arrive in the port city.

When Ahaziah concludes his speech, one by one the newly constructed ships are released from their slips and slide gracefully into the water. Acclamations and cheers resound from the multitudes, and soon the air reverberates with the music of a hundred exuberant performers. The king of Israel declares the start of a feast. The finest wine to be found in the nation is brought to the tables where the dignitaries and officials are proudly seated. All the government officials of note are present, along with military officers and generals. It is a grand moment.

Enter Eliezer

The gaiety of the feast is interrupted, however, by the arrival of Eliezer the prophet. He strides resolutely toward the throne of Jehoshaphat, who senses immediately that the seer's message will be unwelcome.

The man of God points to the king and says, *"Because you have allied yourself with Ahaziah, the LORD has destroyed your works"* (2 Chron. 20:37). The prophet turns around and, with calm dignity, departs.

Ahaziah, greatly embarrassed, speaks up, "Ah, what can be done with fanatics like that one? Their words only serve to frighten the people."

Hours later, dense and menacing clouds gather on the horizon. Soon the wind picks up. Lightening cracks through the sky and thunder echoes in the growing darkness. The seas have grown alarmingly rough even in the shelter of the cove. Huge waves are beating savagely against the rocks of the protecting jetty. The new ships rock violently back and forth as sailors try to save them. The sails are furled tightly and anchors have been cast into the sea, but the angry waves are simply too strong. The ships are crashing against the sharp rocks as if they were mere feathers blown by the breeze.

The next day the sun rises bright and clear. The winds have abated, revealing a clear and calm sky. King Jehoshaphat goes outside and surveys the scene in the harbour. The gala parade stands are heaps of ruin where the flags and banners have been. Everything is in shambles. He staggers down to the beach. Beams of wood and heavy planks bob gently in the now placid waters; the devastation is complete. Worse still, as the king's eyes scan the wreckage, he sees the lifeless bodies of his once proud sailors dotting the beach. His heart is filled with sorrow and regret as he turns and walks away, weeping as a child.

Another Joint Venture?

A year passes and Jehoshaphat begins to build a new fleet. King Ahaziah gains knowledge of the plan and immediately dispatches a royal missive to the king of Judah:

Jehoshaphat: Enemies and Allies

My dear Jehoshaphat,

I have become aware of your plans to construct another flotilla of ships. I sincerely believe this to be a worthy undertaking and that you will enjoy excellent results from this endeavor. Our wise common ancestor, Solomon, had a royal fleet that was of great value to the national economy. I believe the tragedy that befell our former fleet was mere accident due to untimely bad weather, exacerbated by the inexperience of the sailors. Surely such a calamity will not repeat itself. I offer my intimate collaboration in this project and propose that my men work shoulder to shoulder with yours. Together, you and I will undoubtedly achieve notable success.

Humbly yours,
Ahaziah, Great King of Israel

As the messenger finishes reading the letter, Jehoshaphat looks down at the ground. Abruptly he calls for a scribe, to whom he dictates a response. In firm and clear terms, Jehoshaphat rejects further alliance with the king of Israel. He has learned his lesson. A few months later Ahaziah is dead (1 Kgs. 22:48-51).

The Bible Back-Story

The Battle That Wasn't

The three enemy armies destroyed themselves. Obviously, the hand of the LORD was at work. One possible reason for their self-annihilation is that they became confused among themselves; each of them thought that their allies were in fact their enemies. Alternatively it has been proposed that the attacking forces had assumed an easy victory and had decided that it would be better to share the spoils of war between just two rather than among three—and thus sought to eliminate one other. This same process would then be repeated among the two surviving armies.

Yet another suggestion is that the enemy armies were destroyed through the intervention of angelic beings.[1,2]

King Jehoshaphat's men spent three days recovering the spoils of war. The most likely reason for this bounty is that many of the soldiers were mercenaries and carried all their possessions with them.

Ammon and Moab were kingdoms located to the east of the river Jordan and the Dead Sea. Edom was located to the southeast. Engedi is located approximately twenty three miles (as the crow flies) from Jerusalem, near the western shore of the Dead Sea.

Sea-Worthy Facts

The city of Tarshish is near the present location of Cádiz, Spain. Some scholars believe, however, that the term *tarshish* refers not as much to a geographical location as to a type of high-seas vessel. "Ships such as those that traveled to Tarshish were of a construction suitable for long voyages."[3]

There is likewise some difference of opinion as to the location of Ophir. Some have proposed a location in southern Arabia. Others suggest its whereabouts in either Egypt or Somalia (Barton Payne) or even in India.[4]

Ezion Geber, where the first fleet was constructed, lies approximately two miles northeast of Aquaba.

The Struggles in Our Lives

Learn from Jehoshaphat's Prayer

Jehoshaphat's prayer is short but beautiful. The prayer is composed of questions posed to God, almost as if the king were trying to remind the Lord of His promises and of the reasons for which He had made them. Jehoshaphat's words reveal to us a man who has faith in God. His first question deals with the authority of God over the universe. *"Are you not God in heaven, and do You not rule over all the kingdoms of the nations, and in Your*

Jehoshaphat: Enemies and Allies

hand is there not power and might, so that no one is able to withstand You?" (2 Chron. 20:6). Thus Jehoshaphat affirms the strength and might of God. He is not a deity with limited power as the false gods worshipped by the neighboring nations. He is a God who is irresistible and all-powerful.

Next, Jehoshaphat recounts God's past promises, as if He needed to be reminded! *"Are you not our God, who drove out the inhabitants of this land before Your people Israel, and gave it to the descendants of Abraham Your friend forever?"* (2 Chron. 20:7).

Jehoshaphat continues by explaining how His people had *"built You a sanctuary for Your name"* (2 Chron. 20:8). The promise on which the king bases his request is found in the following verse, *"If disaster comes upon us…we will stand before this temple and in Your presence…and You will hear and save"* (2 Chron. 20:9). At this point, Jehoshaphat names their enemies—the people of Ammon, Moab, and Mount Seir and pleads, *"O our God, will You not judge them? For we have no power against this great multitude that is coming against us; nor do we know what to do, but our eyes are upon you"* (2 Chron. 20:12).

The prayer ends by his acknowledging that dependence on God as his only hope. In the past, the king had sought war (2 Chron. 18:3), but now it had come out to meet him. In the Lord, he was ready for it.

Know Your Enemy

Jehoshaphat was totally dependent on God but also totally aware of his enemy. Or, as he experienced, three enemies.

At times we, like Jehoshaphat, feel that we have more than one enemy. The classic list of what confronts the believer names the world, the flesh, and the devil. Yet there are other antagonists. Sometimes we make the opposition to be greater than it really is; at other times the opposition is indeed enormous. Adversaries includes chronic illness, loneliness, lack of affection, financial difficulties. The list could go on. Every human being will be confronted by at least some of these enemies during his or her life.

Our Struggle with Good & Evil

Listen and Act

Jahaziel gave Jehoshaphat God's orders: *"Position yourselves, stand still and see the salvation of the LORD"* (2 Chron. 20:17). Although soldiers are in position and no longer marching forward, they may still be quite nervous and agitated.

To be still and quiet in spirit reminds us of David, who in a similar situation patiently waited for the sound of marching in the mulberry trees (1 Chron. 14:14). This attitude of observation, careful attention, and patient waiting is essential, even when the final result is assured (2 Cor. 2:14).

Getting Ship-Shape

We have all had shipwrecks in our lives, decisions we deeply regret. Some have had "sinkings" that are relatively minor. Perhaps the "ship" wasn't that big or the mistakes that grave. These individuals can recover from the loss and perhaps with time forget the bad experience. Others have had major shipwrecks. Their crises have been so profound that they may never be able to entirely recover.

It is important to note how the shipwreck in Jehoshaphat's life developed. He was a pious man, one of the best kings ever to rule over Judah. His weak point was that he associated with bad company, especially with wicked king Ahab and, after him his son Ahaziah.

Jehoshaphat's recurring mistake was in allying himself with ungodly men. The apostle Paul speaks clearly about the danger of doing so.

Do not be unequally yoked together with unbelievers. For what fellowship has righteousness with lawlessness? And what communion has light with darkness? And what accord has Christ with Belial? Or what part has a believer with an unbeliever? And what agreement has the temple of God with idols? For you are the temple of the living God. As God has said:

Jehoshaphat: Enemies and Allies

"I will dwell in them
And walk among them.
I will be their God,
And they shall be My people."

2 Corinthians 6:14-16

May we as Christians learn this life-lesson before we also suffer a shipwreck!

Do God's Work

There is much for which we may extol Jehoshaphat. His contributions can be measured not only by his devotion, his prayers, and his response to military crises, but also by his concern for the social welfare of his people.

Probably one of the most important aspects of Jehoshaphat's reign was the establishment of a judiciary system accessible to all the citizens of the nation. Without a principled judiciary a nation suffers greatly. Not having easy access to the courts or legal process is an indirect method of depriving citizens of their rights. Jehoshaphat knew this and was probably one of the most notable protagonists of legal reform in the entire history of the Hebrew nation.

We can also collaborate with God's purposes by investing in His future work. Jehoshaphat's twenty-five year reign had a hugely positive spiritual impact on the nation during his time, and in the years to come. Especially noteworthy is that during his administration three prophets arose who would later have an important influence: Micaiah, Jahaziel, and Eliezer.

Using Our Gifts

Commander-in-Chief

Jehoshaphat is presented as an exemplary leader. In a moment of crisis he knew what to do, that is, he knew where to go to have an unsolvable difficulty resolved. He may have felt fear and uncertainty, but he sought the One who is able to overcome fear.

Never in the history of Judah was there a king who was such an optimist regarding his nation's military capability. But this was not based on superficial enthusiasm or without reason. The spiritual leader needs to have a contagious optimism that is based on reality and trusts in the blessing of God.

The king personally encouraged his troops and after all had gone forth out Jerusalem he assumed the lead position. Everyone recognized that he was exceedingly brave (2 Chron. 18:3). The good leader does not leave to his subordinates what he knows is his duty, even though it may involve risk.

Choose Your Allies Carefully

Partnerships or associations with those who have no fear of God, or who actually are openly against the things of God, can never receive the blessing of the Lord (2 Cor. 6:14-15). Jehoshaphat learned this lesson the hard way.

In today's church there may be a temptation to admit leaders or other assistants into the church who do not absolutely share in our Christian principles. The spiritual leader will not give his approbation to such a plan. Again, the counseling of a married couple by a humanist psychologist who denies the authority of the Bible cannot be the solution of choice by the church or of a Bible-believing organization.

Jehoshaphat erred seriously in this regard and the result was an entire flotilla of ships destroyed. Nevertheless he eventually learned his lesson and refused any new enterprises with the godless king of Israel. Likewise, today's leaders must listen to godly counsel, learn from their mistakes, and be committed not to repeat the error.

Comparisons, Contrast and Ideas to Expand

The message of the Prophet Jahaziel (2 Chron. 20)	The message of Paul
Be not afraid (v. 15)	You did not receive the spirit of fear (Rom. 8:15).

Jehoshaphat: Enemies and Allies

The message of the Prophet Jahaziel (2 Chron. 20)	The message of Paul
Be not dismayed (v. 15)	Since we have this ministry, we do not lose heart (2 Cor. 4:1).
The battle is of God (v. 15)	We are more than conquerors (Rom. 8:31)
You will not need to fight (v 17)	Our battle is not against flesh and blood (Eph. 6:12).
See the salvation of the Lord (v 17)	The God of peace will crush Satan under your feet shortly (Rom. 16:20).
Tomorrow go out against them (v 17)	It is high time to awake out of sleep (Rom. 13:11)
The Lord is with you (v 17)	The Lord stood with me and…delivered me out of the mouth of the lion (2 Tim. 4:17)

Ships and Storms

- *"The Perfect Storm"* (Ps. 107:23-30)
- Jehoshaphat's destroyed ships (2 Chron. 20:37)
- Jonah, the storm and the ship that almost sank (Jon. 1:4)
- The capsizing that didn't happen—the boat in which the disciples traveled on the stormy night on the Sea of Galilee (Matt. 8:25)
- Paul's shipwreck experiences (Acts. 27:44)
- The worst shipwreck of all: Lives made shipwreck; Hymenaeus and Alexander (1 Tim. 1:19)

Discussion Starters

1. What attributes of God are seen in these two accounts from Jehoshaphat's life?

2. What fresh truths can we learn from the model prayer uttered by Jehoshaphat if we compare it to Hebrews 4:14-16?

3. What principles might Jehoshaphat tell us about choosing allies?

4. Assign the following "ship stories" to group members. What key truth do you take from "The Perfect Storm" (Ps 107:23-30); Jonah and the near-shipwreck (Jonah 1); Jesus and the disciples the Sea of Galilee (Matt 8:23-27); and Paul's shipwreck en route to Rome (Acts 27)?

5. Why do you think Paul chose a shipwreck metaphor in 1 Timothy 1:18-20?

Chapter 8

JOASH AND AMAZIAH: IS GOD IN CONTROL?

It was the day on which the Spirit of God came upon Zechariah. On a raised platform, the priest of God stood before the king of Judah and his royal ministers. The people of Jerusalem gathered below.

Joash Dances with Wolves

A Warning from God

Joash had long known Zechariah, whose mother saved the king's life when wicked Queen Athaliah sought to eliminate the entire royal family. Joash was a young boy when he became king; Zechariah's father, chief priest Jehoiada, was his godly regent and father-figure for many years (2 Chron. 22:10-23:3).

As the ruler watched Zechariah ascend the platform that had been constructed in the broad temple courtyard, he reflected on the reason the convocation had been called. Several months previously the nobles of Judah had asked for greater tolerance and more religious liberty regarding worship services. Even King Joash, once a faithful defender of the Lord's work, had become spiritually neglectful (2 Chron. 24:15-19).

Now, as Zechariah raises his hands, the multitude grows quiet. With a firm voice he declares, *"Thus says God..."* (2 Chron. 24:20).

It had been a long time since the people heard such solemn words. Many had concluded that God was aloof and uninterested in the affairs of man. They felt as if their everyday dealings, and even their transgressions, were unimportant or unnoticed.

The priest continues, "Why have you broken the commandments of the Lord?"

There is total silence. No one dares reply. King Joash, however, grows increasingly angry and begins to grind his teeth.

"Then the Spirit of God came upon Zechariah the son of Jehoiada the priest, who stood above the people, and said to them, 'Thus says God: "Why do you transgress the commandments of the Lord, so that you cannot prosper? Because you have forsaken the Lord, He also has forsaken you."'" (2 Chron. 24:20).

The king is irate, certain that the old priest's words will squelch the optimistic spirit of the nation. The morale of his army will suffer if his officers listen to such depressing admonitions. Doesn't the old man know that all that talk about the people abandoning God and God abandoning them is immensely discouraging?

A few days later, the princes of Judah come to speak with the king. "Your Majesty, the priest Zechariah has grown annoyingly impertinent. How dare he preach against our freedom to worship as we see fit."

The king hesitates to concur with the princes, but neither does he dare to defend Zechariah. In fact, the monarch has come to regard his old friend as a nuisance, but one who will not be easy to eliminate. Many people highly respect Zechariah and admire his dedication and service to God. Yet something must be done...

Zechariah has been brought to the court in front of the temple to be judged. Several false witnesses come forward and present testimony in which they twist and distort the old priest's words. They suggest that he has committed crimes against Moses by warning that God would forsake His chosen people.

Joash and Amaziah: Is God in Control?

In all this Zechariah does not back down. He has been falsely accused of betraying the nation, of fanaticism, and of extremism. He was ordered to retract his words of warning but refuses to do so. Instead, he resumes his place in front of the temple and reiterates God's message, speaking loudly and clearly for all the people to hear.

King Joash hesitates, remembering his history with Zechariah and his family. Finally he concludes that if the princes withdraw their support from him, his reign would surely fall. He seems to hear a voice in his head whispering, "You must think of the kingdom first, come what may." At the king's signal, all the hatred and evil burning in the hearts of those opposed to Zechariah boils over. The people rush forward and shove the old man to the ground. They pick up heavy rocks and heave them in vengeance on the fallen priest. With his dying breath Zechariah declares, *"The LORD look on it, and repay!"* (2 Chron. 24:22).

Joash issues strict orders to which he demands immediate obedience. "Take away his body and bury it. Clean up this floor until there is not a stain left. Nothing has happened here!" Ironically, the body of Zechariah lies just a short distance from where Zechariah's mother, at the risk of her life, had hidden the child Joash as a prince and saved him from certain death.

Facing the True Enemy

A year has now passed. The king is informed that the Syrian army has marched toward Judah. He urgently orders his men to prepare for battle. At a meeting of his commanders, Joash anxiously inquires about the tactics of the enemy and its strength.

"There is no cause for worry," one of them replies. "We have information that the enemy forces are limited. We should encounter no problems in dealing with their army."

"Then let us teach those Syrians a lesson!"

Little did Joash know that God had abandoned him, as Zechariah had prophesied.

The battle against the Syrians ends with the complete defeat of the army of Judah. One by one the princes who had conspired against Zechariah are felled by the enemy's sword (2 Chron. 24:23). When the king of Syria arrives in Jerusalem, Joash is left with no alternative but to give him all the gold and silver that can be found in the temple (2 Kgs. 12:18).

Joash has learned an exceedingly painful lesson. The Lord is the one who gives the victory. Without Him there can be no success.

The battle has left the king in an extremely vulnerable condition. While lying in his bed seeking to recover, two of his servants enter his room and kill him. His life ends as violently as the priest's.

Amaziah, Son of Joash

War with Edom

"Your highness," reports one of the leading generals of the Judean army despairingly, "we will need an additional one hundred thousand men to match the strength of the enemy army of Edom."

While King Amaziah contemplates the general's grim assessment, another advisor speaks up. "Your Majesty, for one hundred talents of silver we can obtain the service of the Israelite regiments to aid us in the campaign."

In desperation, the king quickly agrees to the plan and the silver is duly dispatched to Judah's neighbor to the north, the kingdom of Israel.

Months pass before the brave but poorly disciplined Israelite soldiers arrive. With only days remaining before the combined Israeli-Judean armies go to battle, a courageous prophet appears before Amaziah. The message from God is succinct: *"O king, do not let the army of Israel go with you, for the LORD is not with Israel... God shall make you fall before the enemy"* (2 Chron. 25:7-8).

Joash and Amaziah: Is God in Control?

The king is incredulous. "Are you trying to tell me that one hundred thousand combat soldiers will not make a difference in the battle?"

The servant of God replies reassuringly, "*God has power to help and to overthrow*" (2 Chron. 25:8)

The king is in a quandary, but after long deliberation he concedes to the prophet, "You have convinced me. But the idea of having wasted so much money is appalling."

"The LORD is able to give you much more than this" (2 Chron. 25:9)

With a word the ruler dismisses the troops of Israel. The Israelite officers and soldiers retire from the field offended and angry. They had been expecting a quick victory followed by extensive plundering of the defeated enemy. Amaziah then orders his remaining Judean soldiers to battle against Edom (Seir) and enjoys a resounding victory. Ten thousand of the enemy are killed.

Meanwhile the dismissed troops of Israel take advantage of the absence of the Judean army. They have dedicated themselves to the sacking of Judean cities. In their looting spree they kill more than three thousand people.

Spoiled by Spoils

Returning to Jerusalem, Amaziah carefully examines the spoils of war he has won. He is awed by the craftsmanship of the pagan idols, images of mythological deities with the head of one animal and the body of another. The more Amaziah scrutinizes the effigies, the more he is fascinated. Many are fashioned of pure gold or silver; others, of the finest ivory. Satanic idols worshiped for centuries by the Edomites are now in the king's possession. Visions of them appear in his mind time after time through the day. Then, on a gray and rainy afternoon, as if pulled by an invisible, powerful force, Amaziah returns to the storage house where he has placed the pagan idols. There he kneels before them, burns incense, and worships (2 Chron. 25:14).

Thunder cracks through the sky and rain falls heavily, as though the heavens were weeping. The anger of the Lord is aroused against Amaziah, and He sends another of His servants. The prophet demands, *"Why have you sought the gods of the people, which could not rescue their own people from your hand?"* (2 Chron. 25:15).

The ruler fires back, "Have we made you the king's counselor? Cease! Don't make me do to you what my father did to Zechariah."

Not intimidated into silence, the brave prophet points at Amaziah and exclaims, *"I know that God has determined to destroy you, because you have done this and have not heeded my advice"* (2 Chron. 25:16). He abruptly withdraws from the room.

The king strikes his clenched fist on a nearby table. He is infuriated but lacks the spirit and the will to fulfill his threat against the herald of God. The triumph against Edom had given the king the presumptuous idea that the victory was accomplished by his own army and his personal genius rather than through the intervention of God. Amaziah is convinced he is capable of great achievements. After all, his officers have been extensively trained. He has become intoxicated by the cheap flattery and adulation of those who repeatedly praise him for his brilliant victory and perfect battle strategy.

High-Minded Thistles and Proud Cedars

A few months later Amaziah calls together his commanders and leaders. He has decided to go to war against Jehoash, the King of Israel (2 Kgs. 14:8). Amaziah, a direct descendant of King David, still covets the territory that years ago was lost. A courier is dispatched to the king of Israel with the following message: *"Come, let us face one another in battle"* (2 Kgs. 14:8).

Jehoash is enraged. He rips the message into tiny pieces and disgustedly tosses the scraps into the fire. After some thought, he sends his own emissary with his reply. While Amaziah's letter was brusque and abrupt, Jehoash's reply is a work of literary subtlety.

Joash and Amaziah: Is God in Control?

Receiving Jehoash's letter, Amaziah orders his secretary to read it in his presence. The response is curious, both a fable and a parable at the same time. *"The thistle that was in Lebanon sent to the cedar that was in Lebanon, saying, 'Give your daughter to my son as wife'..."* (2 Kgs. 14:9).

"Your Majesty," the secretary interjects, "consider with what respect the king of Israel compares your strength, might, and greatness to the mighty cedars of Lebanon!"

The naive secretary had missed the enemy's sarcasm, but King Amaziah does not. He grows so angry that his face turns red, and he bellows, "What impudence to call **me** a thistle while comparing **himself** to a mighty cedar!"

The flustered attendant continues reading: *"...and a wild beast that was in Lebanon passed by and trampled the thistle. You have indeed defeated Edom, and your heart has lifted you up. Glory in that, and stay at home; for why should you meddle with trouble so that you fall—you and Judah with you?"* (2 Kings 14:9-10). Amaziah can no longer constrain himself and shouts, "Who is this insolent man? I am the king of Judah! I am a descendant of David and of Solomon! An enormous army is at my command."

The battle between Israel and Judah would be fought at Beth Shemesh. The army of Jehoash soon devastates the army of Amaziah. The men of Judah seem paralyzed; their response to attacks is uncoordinated and ineffective. Fear and panic overcome the soldiers, and tens of thousands of them fall in the battle. King Amaziah himself is captured and taken to his own capital, Jerusalem, which Jehoash triumphantly enters in his war chariot.

Bound by a rope around his neck, Amaziah walks dolefully and submissively, as if he were a dog. The shame of defeat has brought bitter tears to his eyes. He remembers the false gods he had adored and the harsh words of the prophet: *"I know that God has determined to destroy you..."* (2 Chron. 25:16).

Our Struggle with Good & Evil
The Bible Back-Story

The Boy King Grows Up

The leaders of the people (the princes) approached King Joash and confessed their loyalty (2 Chron 24:17). It is likely, however, that their real motivation was not so much to express allegiance as it was to seek permission to worship in their own cities and regions. They would have used the excuse of trying to avoid the journey and associated dangers of travel to Jerusalem to regularly worship God. Such a practice had already been established in Israel. It would have been only natural to later liberalize the concept to include the worship of gods of their choice.

Whether Joash ended his days bedridden because of natural illness or because of wounds suffered at the hands of the Syrians is uncertain. The fact that it is specifically mentioned that the Syrians departed implies that there may have been some form of epidemic or pestilence such as typhus in the land. Epidemics of this sort were common during military campaigns. The Hebrew wording suggests that Joash was suffering from an illness rather than from wounds.

The extent of the crime committed against Zechariah may not have been limited to him alone. The Latin Vulgate translation of the Bible mentions seventy others. It is possible that not only Zechariah died at the hands of the king but also his brothers and fellow priests as well.

A final matter of some uncertainty is the identity of Zechariah, whom Joash condemned to death. According to Eugene Merrill,[1] the priest Zechariah in 2 Chronicles 24 was the son of Berechiah and grandson of Jehoida. Many sources favor a straightforward reading of verse 20, that he was *"the son of Jehoiada the priest."* The least popular theory is that he was the author of the book of the Bible that bears his name.

Amaziah's Army

The decay of the military prowess of the Kingdom of Judah is seen in the minimal number of soldiers who were mustered.

Joash and Amaziah: Is God in Control?

The army of Amaziah numbered three hundred thousand men while his ancestor, Jehoshaphat, numbered more than a million (2 Chron. 17:14-18).

In spite of the reduced numbers, God gave Judah the victory over Edom because of Amaziah's obedience. He then captured the city of Sela (2 Kgs. 14:7), believed to be modern day Petra. The ruins of this city, which can be visited today, are located in almost impregnable canyons.

Following the capture of the city, ten thousand prisoners were barbarously thrown over a steep precipice. This practice, which would horrify us, was common in those days. Matthew Henry has suggested "it would have, perhaps, been better to have thrown into the abyss the idols of the Edomites rather than the poor captives."[2]

In contrast with the glorious win over Edom, the battle against Israel was a disaster for Judah. Josephus indicates that during the battle against King Jehoash a fear fell over the army of Amaziah "of the type which God, when He is discontent, sends upon men." Josephus goes on to say that the King of Judah was taken prisoner and was threatened by Jehoash with death if he did not open the gates of Jerusalem. Jehoash plundered the temple of God, later making a 500-foot breach in the walls of the city through which he drove his chariot with Amaziah alongside as his prisoner.

That the enemy king pardoned Amaziah's life and even permitted him to continue to reign as monarch seems to suggest he had accepted the payment of tribute and perhaps Israelite hegemony. Jehoash took captive to Israel the sons of the Judean nobles, the most educated and influential men of the kingdom (2 Kgs. 14:14).

The Scriptures make frequent reference to spines and thistles, beginning with the curse that fell upon the earth following Adam's sin (Gen. 3:18; Isa. 5:6; Hos. 10:8).

One hundred talents of silver would be equivalent to about thirty-four tons of silver.

Our Struggle with Good & Evil
The Struggles in Our Lives

Start Well, Finish Well

Many men have died in a place associated with sin or vice, but Zechariah died between the altar of the Lord and the sanctuary. The Almighty had given him the privilege of breathing the last breath of his life in the place he loved the most.

The lives of Joash and Zechariah are like a road that for a long time was one but later separates into two diverging paths. In the beginning, the king and the priest had much in common but later their ways divided, significantly and tragically. The path taken by Joash was a treacherous one, which eventually led to a precipitous fall.

What caused a king who started so well to turn away from God? Almost certainly it can be said of him that he had no profound convictions of his own. Like a broom straw he was easily persuaded and bent (Eph. 4:4). Another probable factor in his spiritual decline was the bad example of the priests of God themselves. Certainly their hypocrisy ate away at his own faithfulness to God (2 Chron. 24:6).

Many Christians begin well but may later drift away from God and even fall into serious sin. Joash's tragic departure from God should remind us all of Paul's words, *"Therefore let him who thinks he stands take heed lest he fall"* (1 Cor. 10:12).

Honour Your Spiritual Mentors

Joash began his reign at only seven years of age under the strong guidance and tutelage of Jehoida, the high priest. The influence of that consecrated man on the life of the young monarch is unmistakable.

Joash's first recorded ministry to the Lord was in charging the Levites with collecting funds and offerings for the temple. At thirty years of age Joash takes personal responsibility for the restoration of the place of worship (2 Kgs. 12:6). The spiritual state of Judah had fallen to such depths that the Scriptures state that the Levites themselves gave no diligence in the matter.

Joash and Amaziah: Is God in Control?

Under the auspices of young King Joash, there was a new feeling of enthusiasm among the people of Judah. The temple coffers began to fill rapidly with generous offerings. Joash took the money and personally employed and directed the workmen in the temple's reconstruction. The fervor and integrity of the men involved in the reconstruction effort was such that there was no need to demand an account of the use of the funds. The men worked with total honesty. Finally the day came when the work was finished. The temple had been restored to its former state and thoroughly reinforced (2 Chron. 24:13). The story reaches its climax when the Scriptures declare, *"And they offered burnt offerings in the house of the LORD continually all the days of Jehoida"* (2 Chron. 24:14b).

In spite of the temporary revival, the death of Jehoida presaged the gathering storm clouds. As long as Joash stayed close to Jehoida, he did well. But when the old priest died, things began to unravel. Joash was a man who had no strength of character or moral fiber. He had spiritual initiative only when Jehoida's support was near at hand.

Beware the Slippery Slope

The first hint that things are not going well in the spiritual life of the king is seen in the brusque and rude manner in which, at the age of thirty, he addresses the High Priest and the clergy. Joash practically accuses Jehoida of negligence (2 Kgs. 12:7). His spiritual decline continues until he even gives his assent to the death of Zechariah. The phrase *"they conspired against him"* (2 Chron. 24:21) relative to Zechariah's stoning, seems to indicate premeditation rather than a simple reaction to the priest's speech.

Hebrew tradition holds that seven sins were committed when Joash authorized the killing of Zechariah:

- A priest was murdered.
- A prophet was murdered.
- A judge was murdered.
- Innocent blood was shed.

- The court of the temple was profaned.
- The Sabbath day was profaned.
- The Day of Atonement was profaned (according to tradition, the day on which the assassination took place).

Barton Payne hits the mark when he compares the life of Joash with the history of Israel as a nation.[3] In the beginning Israel was faithful to the Lord. Later, in a gradual but progressive fashion, the nation departs from its heritage. The prophets sent by God to faithfully warn the people are coldly killed. The nation's decay reaches its zenith when Israel crucifies the Messiah. The end is judgment and destruction.

Appreciate God's Grace

The final verdict by which the life of Joash is measured includes this significant qualifying phrase, *"Joash did what was right in the sight of the Lord all the days of Jehoiada the priest"* (2 Chron. 24:2). The biblical assessment of Joash's life demonstrates the grace of God. The right (or the good or the just) that he did is acknowledged, in spite of the great evil he committed at the end of his life.

How precious to know that the Lord in His mercy forgives those who truly repent and return to Him (Isa. 1:18). Probably very few of us would have recognized the good in the life of Joash after he committed such a vile act. The balances God uses to evaluate our lives are very different from our own but always perfect in grace and mercy. Through the Lord's mercies, we are not consumed because His compassion does not fail (Lam. 3:20-21). We should bow gratefully before the Father in thanksgiving for the sanctifying work of the Holy Spirit (John 16:7) and the continual intercession of the Lord Jesus Christ (Heb. 7:25).

Keep Seeking God's Resources

In these glimpses of Amaziah's life, we see that the prophet taught him an essential precept: In God there is power to help. This principle will be further developed by the apostle Paul when he says, *"If God be for us, who can be against us?"* and

Joash and Amaziah: Is God in Control?

afterwards, *"In all these things we are more than conquerors through Him who loved us"* (Rom. 8:31, 37).

The assertion "The LORD is able to give you much more than this" has great practical application today. A believer may commit to a course of action with questionable elements and consequently has nagging doubts whether his or her integrity has been compromised. Everyone is confronted by situations in which it appears that, if we don't seize the moment, we'll never again have such a golden opportunity. For example, a young woman may be considering marriage to a man of doubtful reputation. Perhaps a believer is offered a job with a rewarding salary but in a dubious place of employment. The Christian should remember God is able to provide more abundantly than whatever the world may offer.

Be Open to Godly Counsel

When the first prophet came to him, Amaziah attentively listened to God's message, heeded it, and then dismissed the mercenary aid he had acquired at great cost. When the second prophet, however, warns Amaziah of the sin of bowing before pagan idols, the king gives no regard to the message from God. Instead, he becomes angry and threatens the prophet with death. The third "messenger" to the monarch is the king of Israel, who wisely warns him not to become involved in an unnecessary war. Again, the ruler disregards counsel. Throughout this process one can see the mercy of God as He patiently gives Amaziah three opportunities to change his ways. God is never without His witness.

Later in his life, as a result of his sin of idolatry, *"the anger of God was aroused against Amaziah"* (2 Chron. 25:15). At this juncture, as we have seen, a valiant servant of God approaches the king and predicts his total ruin. Unfortunately, instead of repenting, he threatened the faithful prophet with death.

Humble Yourself

We observe how God uses and arranges events and human decisions in order to fulfill His divine purposes. Amaziah's fall

143

is assured when he, in his pride, provokes King Jehoash to war. He forgot the biblical principle that *"God resists the proud but gives grace to the humble"* (1 Pet. 5:5). He disregarded the wise precept that *"it is honourable for a man to stop striving since any fool can start a quarrel"* (Prov. 20:3).

King Jehoash, knowing little of humility, responds to Amaziah's boisterous threat by declaring *"the thistle that was in Lebanon sent to the cedar that was in Lebanon"* (2 Chron. 25:18). As is common in fables, inanimate objects are given the ability to speak as if they were human. Why would God record in His Word such an unusual message, particularly when it originated with a wicked king? Doubtless it is for our edification (Heb. 2:1). In spite of the source, the words are instructive and the message is simple: pride destroys.

Regrettably Amaziah did not perceive the wisdom behind the insulting message but rather he felt offended and humiliated. How easy it is to react negatively when our pride has been bruised. Hundreds of years later our Saviour would teach us, *"Agree with your adversary quickly, while you are on the way with him"* (Matt. 5:25). It is essential to remember that we can learn much even from our enemies.

But Amaziah is not alone in being caught up with his own supposed greatness. Jehoash is so confident and feels so powerful he advises his rival to "stay at home now." Thus we find two proud individuals: Amaziah, who in the past had been God-fearing and Jehoash, who although he had shown respect to Elisha in a previous moment (2 Kgs. 13:14), had little regard for God.

Repent and Return to God

A past history of faithfulness to the Lord is no guarantee of His present blessing if we fall into willful disobedience and refuse to repent. How distressing it is to see a child of God, who had previously "run well", turn away from God's ways in the manner of Amaziah. From this point on, the king of Judah would suffer one catastrophe after another. By no means are believers exempt from difficulties or even tragedies, but in the midst of tough times we may still enjoy the peace of the Lord if we stay close to Him. *"We will not fear even though the earth be removed"* (Ps. 46:2).

In spite of his failing and sin, the Scriptures say Amaziah *"did what was right in the sight of the LORD"* (2 Chron. 25:2). This strongly suggests the possibility that he repented and returned to the Lord at the end of his life. But to his shame the Scriptures continue, "but not with a loyal heart." Matthew Henry expresses the idea with clarity, "He was not a man of serious piety or devotion...he had no zeal for the exercise of religion. He was not an enemy, but rather a cold and indifferent friend."[4]

With humble hearts we must consider what the final verdict will be concerning our own lives—not with respect to our salvation because that cannot be lost *"And I give them eternal life, and they shall never perish; neither shall anyone snatch them out of My hand"* (John 10:28), but rather with respect to our faithfulness to the Lord.

We also must admire the obedience of the one whom the Lord sent. He acted with great courage, placing his very life in grave danger in order to faithfully convey the message God entrusted to him. May we follow the prophet's example.

Using Our Gifts

Choosing to Be Faithful

King Joash was a leader who needed spiritual support. When this help was removed it produced a catastrophe. Zechariah the priest is presented to us as the true spiritual leader of the nation. He is one of the most prominent examples of those who gave their lives for their faithfulness to the Lord. While he may not have known what was to befall him, he nevertheless resolutely chose to be faithful to God.

Godly Counsel

Offensive action against a militarily superior nation normally would be difficult to justify except for reasons of national defense. It seems the governmental and military ministers in Judah voiced no opposition to Amaziah's schemes. The leader must have realized that any endeavor contrary to the will of God would never prosper. The wise leader will always seek counsel from other godly individuals.

One who leads also must recognize that, if the way that has been taken is too risky or dangerous, it is best to reconsider the situation. Stubbornness should not be confused with perseverance.

Comparisons, Contrast and Ideas to Expand

Zechariah	Stephen
Son of the High Priest	One of the Seven (Acts 6:5).
The Spirit came upon him	Full of faith and the Holy Spirit
His message was of judgment	His message was of judgment (Acts 7:51)
His message resulted in his stoning	His message resulted in his stoning
"The Lord look on it and repay" (2 Chron. 24:22).	*"Lord, do not charge them with this sin"* (Acts 7:60).

Discussion Starters

1. In what specific ways was Jehoiada a godly influence?

2. What different decisions could Joash and Amaziah have made in order to stay faithful to God?

3. What are today's dangers of pride and vanity? of involvement with the occult?

4. Do you believe that God can truly give you more if you trust in Him? What fosters such trust?

Chapter 9

UZZIAH AND JOTHAM: TRUE SUCCESS

"I'll go wherever I want to go!" shouts the king. "I'm the one who gives the orders, and absolutely no one is going to stop me."

Entrances and Exits

The Holy Place

Azariah the High Priest and other clergy try, but fail to prevent King Uzziah from recklessly shoving his way into the temple. The soldiers of the royal guard remain outside and dare not go farther. Azariah and about eighty other priests, however, go in the temple after the king.

"*It is not for you, Uzziah,*" Azariah says firmly, "*to burn incense to the LORD, but for the priests, the sons of Aaron, who are consecrated to burn incense*" (2 Chron. 26:18).

The ruler grasps a censer in his hand. His face turns red with anger; his eyes are like daggers. For the first time in his life someone has dared to stand up to him and tell him no. Azariah continues, "*You shall have no honour from the LORD God*" (2 Chron. 26:18).

As Uzziah rages, the priests draw closer together, sealing off the temple. The king gravely warns them that he could order his soldiers to attack without pity. His facial muscles tighten with fury...but suddenly Uzziah has a strange sensation, a sort of itching. His body feels consumed by a rapidly spreading rash, as if thousands of ants were marching across him and biting his flesh. The king looks around at the priests, and is shocked to see them quickly back away from him. The priests' faces reveal horror and revulsion as they watch the transformation happening before their eyes. Almost in unison the voices cry out, "The king has leprosy! He has become a leper!"

Quickly the king glances down at his hands and sees the unmistakable lesions of leprosy. Then he sees the priests staring at his forehead, where he begins to feel the same strange burning sensation. The sovereign is terrified, so overwhelmed with shock that he can do nothing. Shortly, with the help of Azariah and the priests, Uzziah rushes out of the temple as if escaping from a burning building. He looks at his skin again and realizes the lesions are not only still there, they are spreading. He hastens to the royal palace and bursts into his chamber. The king stares into the huge polished brass plate that he uses for a mirror.

King Uzziah weeps bitterly.

The Prophet Isaiah

Let us use our imagination and picture a scene years later. Isaiah the prophet enters the great hall of the palace and sees the throne from which the king had formerly ruled. Uzziah had been successful in military campaigns and had instituted agricultural reforms bringing prosperity to the nation and stability to the economy. Not even the prince, Jotham, who has inherited his father's right to rule wants to sit on that throne for fear of contracting the dreaded disease of leprosy. Isaiah's mind is filled with images of the sad state of the once proud and powerful monarch who has been reduced to isolation and quarantine.

Many years pass since Uzziah's effrontery resulted in his pathetic condition. One day, the people walking the streets of Jerusalem incline their ears to a strange, mournful sound.

Uzziah and Jotham: True Success

Trumpeters are lined up on the palace wall to announce that the once-proud king is dead. He had reigned for fifty-two years.

When Isaiah hears the news, his thoughts return to the magnificent but empty throne. Time and again he has asked himself how it could be possible for such a godly ruler to have committed such a grievous sin. Later, in the silence of his chambers, Isaiah has an astonishing vision. *"I saw the Lord sitting on a throne, high and lifted up, and the train of His robe filled the temple. Above it stood seraphim; each one had six wings: with two he covered his face, with two he covered his feet, and with two he flew"* (Isa. 6:1-2). The prophet cannot help but remember how King Uzziah covered *his* face with his two hands so that the people could not see his leprosy. Now, the celestial beings have covered their faces not in shame but to honour the One seated on the throne.

Isaiah marvels at what he hears. *"Holy, holy, holy is the LORD of Hosts; the whole earth is full of His glory!"* (Isa. 6:3). Isaiah has seen the glory of the Lord Jesus Christ, as described in John 12:38-41.

Little Was Said...but It Was Good

"Mommy, why do we have to honour the Lord?" inquires the curious son of the queen mother.

"My dear child," she replies with a gentle smile, "my father, who was your grandpa, was a very godly priest. He always taught us that the Almighty loves us very much but that we need to be faithful to Him."

Years have passed and the inquisitive little boy has become Prince Jotham of Judah. The royal family is reeling from the divine discipline with which his father, Uzziah, was afflicted following his grave transgression the dreaded disease of leprosy.

"Uncle Jotham," asks the prince's young nephew, "why can we not see Grandpa?"

He responds, "Because my daddy is not well."

"What's wrong with him? Why can't I play with him or give him a kiss as all my friends do with their grandfathers?"

"Because your grandpa is very sick. The doctors say that his disease is contagious to others."

"What does that mean?" asks the child.

At this point the queen, who had been lounging nearby, walks over and softly rests her hand on the young boy's head. She quietly replies, "It means that if he gets near someone then that person may get the same illness that your grandpa has."

"Grandma," the boy says sniffling, "please tell Grandpa to get well very soon and then I'll give him big hugs and kisses."

Tears flow freely down the cheeks of the queen.

The Bible Back-Story

Earthquakes and Affiliations

The prophets Amos (Amos 1:1) and Zechariah (Zech. 14:5) both mention that an earthquake occurred during the reign of Uzziah. It was apparently of substantial magnitude. Josephus states that the earthquake occurred at the exact moment in which Uzziah tried to offer sacrifice in the temple.

Although the judgment of leprosy that fell upon Uzziah was very severe, it was actually less harsh than the prescribed penalty of death for entering the temple (Num. 18:7). Consider the other people of the Old Testament who were afflicted with leprosy: Miriam, for murmuring against Moses as God's appointed authority (Num. 12:1, 9) and Gehazi, for greed (2 Kgs. 5:27). There is no mention of leprosy as a punishment in the New Testament, but there is chastening by means of other illnesses. Paul, for example, writes, *"For this reason many are weak and sick among you, and many sleep"* (1 Cor. 11:30).

The Scriptures reveal various forms of medical afflictions and illnesses that the Lord has used for discipline or chastisement. Nebuchadnezzar suffered from a case of transitory dementia (Dan. 4:33). Ananias and Sapphira were struck with immediate death (Acts 5:1-11). King Herod was judged by a sudden, fatal sickness (Acts 12:23).

Uzziah and Jotham: True Success

Lockyer supposes that Uzziah could have passed the rest of his days taking care of his livestock and his farms, activities he much enjoyed.[1] If this were so, then Uzziah was not absolutely confined to his house (2 Kgs. 26:11). Ultimately the king died at the age of sixty-eight. Rossier concludes his discussion of Uzziah by stating that "it is true that this king who was faithful in the beginning later became a transgressor. He was severely judged while on earth as if being saved from fire."[2]

The Reign of Jotham

Jotham was crowned at the age of twenty-five. He governed the nation for a mere sixteen years prior to his death at forty-one years of age. In contrast, his father, Uzziah, began his reign at sixteen and continued to reign in one of the longest administrations in the history of Judah, fifty-two years.

We do not know how old Uzziah was when he committed the sin resulting in his illness. Leprosy is a chronic disease; he could have lived between ten and twenty years before finally succumbing. Jotham was probably an adolescent when King Uzziah developed leprosy, making it often necessary for the prince to act in his father's place. Undoubtedly the disciplinary experience of his father had a positive result on him. Jotham thus grew up not only as one who loved the Lord, but at the same time as one who had a profound and healthy fear of God.

The Struggles in Our Lives

The Problem of Pride

Uzziah was able to conquer all his military enemies. He was able to rebuild his nation after suffering the enormous damages of a huge earthquake. He had carefully avoided the sins of impurity. In contrast with the kings of neighboring Israel, he was never guilty of having worshiped pagan idols. But he failed in one important point—he couldn't control his pride.

We must consider the story of Uzziah with a sense of warning and a certain degree of fear. This was a man whom God had prospered. He was a person who possessed great talent and leadership skills. But sadly the Scriptures record that his heart was lifted up to his destruction.

Uzziah knew that the kings of the nations of that region often acted as priests, invoking a certain "divine" right. It would seem that he had mistakenly assumed that he too had a special prerogative. Doubtlessly he looked at himself and thought, "I'm just as good as or better than those priests and Levites" (Luke 18:11).

At times we too may make dangerous assumptions concerning our privileges. We may be inclined to believe that because of our faithfulness and steadfastness God will provide us with special treatment and overlook certain questionable attitudes or activities in our lives. But the Scriptures clearly declare that there is no partiality with God (Rom. 2:11).

Uzziah's sin was committed in a public manner and so God disciplined His child in a manner that would likewise be public. Uzziah had sought honour and privilege but received instead dread and revulsion from all who saw him. The great king came to envy the good health of the lowliest and humblest of his servants.

The king had ignored the biblical principle that the Lord in His providence has set limits. When those limits are disregarded the punishment can be severe indeed (Num. 16:32; Acts 5:9). The ruler would certainly have known that the Bible restricts the offering of sacrifices to the Levites and priests alone (Ex. 39:7-8) and he was surely aware that the punishment for transgression was death (Num. 18:7). By going brashly forward with his own desire to sacrifice to God he showed that he had completely lost his reverential fear of the Lord.

The contrast in attitude between Uzziah and Isaiah is notable. Uzziah entered the Holy Place of God with little regard for his own sinful and willfully rebellious condition. Isaiah, on the other hand, upon seeing the vision of the heavenly throne immediately recognized his own sinful state (Isa. 6:5).

Uzziah and Jotham: True Success

The Fear of God

Occasionally an unbalanced focus on certain of God's attributes while minimizing the importance of others of His attributes (such as His holiness) has resulted in a lack of a reverential fear of the Lord. Uzziah attempted to enter the temple of God as if he had as much right to enter it as he had any ordinary building. Similarly today there may sometimes be a lack of reverence upon entering a church building. Times have changed since the days of our grandparents who would demonstrate the utmost respect for the place where the Word of God was preached. It is now fashionable in many places to attend meetings of the church as if it were no different than going to a sports club.

At the beginning of his public life, Uzziah seemed to have had the proverbial Midas touch. His life was characterized by triumph and success in whatever endeavor he undertook. His military campaigns were crowned with victory wherever he went. Uzziah's success was due to his seeking after God even from the days of his youth (2 Chron. 26:5). It was God who was abundantly prospering his life and reign. When the Lord blesses our lives, how easy it is for us to come to believe that we have achieved greatness and success by our own abilities and talents.

The Bible tells us that Uzziah did that which was right in the sight of the LORD according to all that his father Amaziah had done (2 Kgs. 15:4). During the time of the ministry of Zachariah the priest, Uzziah sought after God. As long as his mentor lived, Uzziah did well. He did not follow the Lord merely to seek material blessings for himself but rather because he honestly desired to please God. Some have called this period in Uzziah's reign, a spiritual "Indian summer" for the nation of Judah. It was a time of great blessing but judgment was soon to come.

Build on Your Strengths

In 2 Chronicles 26, Uzziah is presented to us as a man with diverse and unusual abilities. There are numerous intermingling aspects to his life, which may be enumerated as follows.

First (2 Chron. 26:2-5), we have Uzziah presented as **restorer.** He rebuilt Elath, a coastal town in the south of Judah;

he did right in the sight of the Lord; he sought God in the days of Zechariah; and God made him prosper.

The second aspect emphasizes Uzziah's **military ability**. He undertakes campaigns against different kingdoms and wins (2 Chron. 26:6); God helped him against the Philistines, against the Arabians, and against the Menuites (2 Chron. 26:7); and he became exceedingly strong (2 Chron. 26:8).

In the third aspect (2 Chron. 26:10), we see Uzziah as **architect and agriculturalist**. He built towers in the desert; he dug wells for his many livestock; he had farmers and vinedressers in the mountains; and he loved the soil.

The next aspect shows us Uzziah as **commander-in-chief** (2 Chron. 26:11-15). He raises a great army; he develops the use of military equipment, including the catapult; and his fame spread far and wide as he became strong (2 Chron. 26:15).

Boast in the Lord

If the story of Uzziah had ended with verse fifteen we would have thought him to be one of the greatest and most successful kings of Judah. The verse which reveals his tragic fall is solemn: *"But when he was strong his heart was lifted up, to his destruction, for he transgressed against the LORD his God by entering the temple of the LORD to burn incense on the altar of incense"* (2 Chron. 26:16).

Even the believer who is honestly trying to follow the Lord must be ever vigilant to avoid both boasting of success in ministry and considering a spiritual gift from the Lord as his own ability (1 Cor. 9:15-18). Yet, the believer can well sing a song of hallelujah to the Saviour, because failure is by no means unavoidable. The book of Revelation abounds with the phrase *"to him who overcomes"* (for example Rev. 2:17; 2:26; 3:21). Certainly this triumphal expression indicates that victory is possible. The Lord has given us instruments, or more biblically, *"spiritual weapons,"* by means of which we may prevail in life (Eph. 6:11-17).

The believer's sins, while ultimately forgiven of the Lord, may nevertheless result in consequences that endure. The

Uzziah and Jotham: True Success

Scriptures state that Uzziah was a leper until the day of his death. There is no mention of prayer for his healing. The situation is similar to that mentioned by the Apostle John: *"There is a sin leading to death. I do not say that he should pray about that"* (1 John 5:16).

The final analysis of Uzziah's life, though, was that he did right in the eyes of the LORD. What's more, when speaking of Uzziah's son Jotham, the Bible says he *"did what was right in the sight of the LORD, according to all that his father Uzziah had done (although he did not enter the temple of the LORD)"* (2 Chron. 27:2). Jotham had learned from his father's mistake, seen the resulting punishment, and did not commit the same error.

Lessons from Jotham

The Scriptures paint but a brief portrait of the life of Jotham, focusing on two principal aspects. He is compared to his father who *"did what was right in the sight of the LORD according to all that his father Uzziah had done"* but the text immediately makes the distinction, *"although he did not enter the temple of the Lord"* (2 Chron. 27:2).

As is true with all of us, the young king was not without his difficulties. In his case he had to cope with the emotional agony of having a family member, his own father, close by but unable to approach him because of his contagious and incurable illness. How difficult it must have been to be unable to even come near to one whom he loved so much, and by whom he was loved.

The account of King Jotham confronts us with the delicate subject of dealing with those having serious, contagious diseases. In Jotham's day, leprosy and tuberculosis were among the most dreaded chronic diseases. In today's world the problem of AIDS has resulted in a great deal of social isolation. The pathology of the disease is well known having been extensively studied, but the social consequences resulting from the fear of contracting the illness are strong nevertheless.

Jotham was a man dedicated to architecture and engineering. He constructed the upper part of the Ophel wall in Jerusalem. He was also responsible for the strengthening of the nation's defenses by building fortresses and defensive towers in the mountain regions and forests of the land. In addition, Jotham undertook a military campaign against Ammon in which he proved victorious. As a result of his success, the enemy was forced to pay an annual levy of silver as well as a tribute of their agricultural produce. Other minor campaigns are likewise mentioned (2 Chron. 27: 7).

In spite of these notable achievements, Jotham's life was characterized by neither extensive military undertakings nor grandiose building projects. Jotham's fundamental motivation was to please God. He was so conscious of divine holiness that he constantly scrutinized his ways in order to avoid offending the Omnipotent. The only fault to be found was the raising of his son, who was to later assume the throne. The Scriptures record that his son, Ahaz, *"did not do what was right in the sight of the LORD"* (2 Chron. 28:1). Sadly, Jotham was but forty-one years old when he suffered a "premature" death. Ahaz was left with neither a father nor a grandfather to nurture, discipline, and guide him. Interestingly, Jotham's grandchild, Hezekiah, proved to be one of the godliest of the kings of Judah (2 Chron. 29:2).

Using Our Gifts

Three Different Leaders

In 2 Chronicles 26 we find three distinct groups of leaders. First, there is a spiritual leader named Zechariah, who was a beneficial influence in the young king's life. As a result of that influence, King Uzziah enjoyed true spiritual growth.

Second, we have the leadership of King Uzziah, during the days in which he sought the Lord. His leadership was displayed in various areas. He ably directed military campaigns against the enemies surrounding Judah. He was also noted for constructing emplacements, defensive works to protect his country, and for the development of agriculture.

Third, we have the noteworthy leader Azariah, considered to be the high priest. This man fulfilled his duty, even risking

Uzziah and Jotham: True Success

his life, in order to deny King Uzziah entrance to the temple. The historian Josephus[3] tells us that King Uzziah threatened the priests with death if they did not permit him to enter. It is praiseworthy that eighty priests accompanied their superior in an undertaking that could have cost them their lives.

Seeking God

Every time we undertake a new project or endeavor we should diligently seek the direction of the Lord. Jotham's life reaffirms the blessings resulting from this attitude: *"So Jotham became mighty, because he prepared his ways before the LORD his God"* (2 Chron. 27:6).

Jotham had learned the importance of not transgressing the commandments of the Lord. Both violating prohibitions and failing to obey obligations can have grave consequences. Many of Jotham's ancestors as well as his successors believed erroneously that, if they were strong militarily, they would have national security. In contrast, Jotham had clearly learned that success rests not on outward strength or power but on having the blessings of God.

Discussion Starters

1. How did Uzziah's divine punishment affect his son Jotham?

2. How susceptible are we to committing the same sin as Uzziah's?

3. Why does God sometimes give to relatively good and righteous people, such as Jotham, such short lives?

4. What is the relationship between faithfulness to God and success in life?

5. What is more important to national security, military strength or moral integrity?

Part 3

THE UPS AND DOWNS
OF THE CROWN

Chapter 10

HEZEKIAH: THE BEST OF THEM?

"Break it up with hammers! Slice it apart with saws! Eliminate the remains with fire!"

Crush the Serpent

Whom Do You Worship?

Royal ministers, priests, and Levites watch in anger and disgust. Some shout their protests. King Hezekiah is ordering the destruction of the sacred bronze serpent of Moses.

The ruler responds, "I want it broken up...and then completely destroyed!"

The hammers ring out anew as the heavy blows strike hard against huge sharpened chisels. Sparks fly into the air. The head of the serpent proves especially resistant. At length, though, the sculpture has been reduced to a pile of unrecognizable bronze filings and chips (2 Kgs. 18:4-8).

Several days later Hezekiah calls together the priests and Levites. The religious men gather together in the eastern plaza of the temple mount. From his position atop a high platform, the king addresses the assembled men. Many have become spiritually very cold; only a few remain faithful to the Lord. The temple itself is essentially abandoned (2 Chron. 29:4-11).

Clearly and firmly the king admonishes, "My sons, do not be negligent concerning your spiritual duties. Jehovah has chosen you to stand before Him."

One of the priests nudges the man next to him and says, "How is that going to put food on the table? We're asked to do a lot but where are the offerings?"

The monarch continues, "You know what a great distinction and honour it is to be before the king. But the Lord has given you the privilege of standing before God Himself, the One who is the King of kings."

Some of the men begin to shake their heads as if to say, "Sure, that's all well and good, but it doesn't help me any. I wonder if I shouldn't take up some secular profession" (Mal. 3:14).

Raising his voice, Hezekiah says, "Now serve Him and minister to Him. You are ministers of the King of Glory, a privilege that is immeasurably great!"

The ruler finishes his speech and slowly steps down from the platform.

True Reform

The doors of the temple had been closed for many years. When they are finally opened a nauseating odor escapes from the dark, long-neglected interior, and the sun's rays enter — symbolic of letting the light of revival cleanse the building of the nation's corruption. *"In the first year of his reign, in the first month,* [Hezekiah] *opened the doors of the house of the LORD and repaired them"* (2 Chron. 29:3). Crossing the threshold, the priests find the lamps darkened. They were to have been kept burning continuously (2 Chron. 29:7).

What the religious men found inside was heartrending. The temple was to have been a building consecrated to Almighty God, but the great chamber was filled with every kind of diabolical image and horrendous object related to idol worship. The king shivered at the sight of the depth of abomination to which the temple had degenerated. It was as if a surgeon were to enter an operating room expecting to find everything completely spotless and sterile, instead, discovering it not only filthy but full of putrefaction and brimming with the most virulent strains of deadly germs. Yet how insufficient is such a simile when we contemplate the repugnant, sacrilegious idols found in the temple of the Most Holy God. The priests *"brought out all the debris that they found in the temple of the LORD to the court of the house of the LORD. And the Levites took it out and carried it to the Brook Kidron"* (2 Chron. 29:16b).

Months pass. King Hezekiah continues to seek the Lord and in every way please Him. Now an enormous multitude has come to Jerusalem from all the regions of Judah and even from different parts of the kingdom of Israel. In the courtyard of the temple, the priests prepare themselves for the sacrifices in accordance with the law. There is an atmosphere of joy and anticipation that pervades the setting. The streets are filled with the music of instruments and singing as the people raise their voices in praise to the Lord (2 Chron. 29:27). The time has come for the sacrifice of the burnt offering. The monarch and his entourage kneel down and worship God. Hezekiah tells the Levites, *"Now that you have consecrated yourselves to the LORD, come near, and bring sacrifices and thank offerings into the house of the LORD"* (2 Chron. 29:31).

Hundreds of years later the apostle Peter would write, *"You also, as living stones, are being built up a spiritual house, a holy priesthood, to offer up spiritual sacrifices acceptable to God through Jesus Christ"* (1 Pet. 2:5).

"Look at All My Gold!"

A Guided Tour

"Follow us, my esteemed ambassadors. Walk through here, please."

Now an older man, King Hezekiah is dazzling in his finest clothing. He wears the royal crown on his head. High officials of Judah accompany him on either side. The Babylonian ambassadors are elegantly dressed as well.

"Your Majesty," says one of the delegates of the diplomatic mission, "we were saddened to know that your Excellency was ill, but relieved to hear of your extraordinary recovery. We'd like to offer our most sincere wishes for your peace and health. Our king conveys his special respects. He has also sent you this humble gift."

With those words the ambassador's attendant steps forward with trays of jewelry of gold and precious stones. The Jewish officials are in awe. King Hezekiah orders the gems of greatest value be shown to all the highest-ranking officials present. The jewelry had been crafted by the best artisans in the world. Later, after a long discussion—with frequent use of words such as *peace, understanding, treaty, friendship,* and *brotherhood*—Hezekiah speaks. "Yes, it's true I was very ill, almost to the point of death. But the Lord God of Israel had mercy on me. He performed a miracle and cured me."

In the days that follow, the monarch shows the visitors the treasures of his kingdom. His years of prosperity have permitted him to accumulate great wealth. Hezekiah takes his visitors first to the chambers of the royal treasury, where ingots of gold and silver are carefully arranged and stored. The ambassadors don't hide their satisfaction and repeatedly congratulate the king for having such valuable holdings. Later they see quantities of cut gems and all types of ornaments of silver, gold, and marble.

The next day, the ruler shows his guests stores of perfumes and ointments. These have been brought from different kingdoms of the surrounding areas and are all of the highest quality. King Hezekiah seems to be like a child in the way he delights in seeing the diplomats' reactions to his wealth.

"Please, sniff this Arabian perfume…Just take a whiff of this ointment from Egypt…Can you smell the aroma of this balm from Sheba?"

A few days later, Hezekiah takes the delegation to a large, strongly-guarded building. Before entering, the king assumes a theatrical stance as if the scene were to be televised. "Honoured ambassadors from the great kingdom of Babylonia, what you are about to see I have never shown to anyone. It is a state secret. But because you are friends and because we have signed a treaty of peace, cooperation, and mutual non-aggression, it is my privilege to reveal it to you."

The Babylonian officials enter the building and see that it is filled with various kinds of armaments. "Your highness," says the highest ranking of them, "we are amazed to see the vastness of the armaments of your kingdom. These weapons are of the highest quality. Our king will greatly esteem being able to number Judah among his allies, particularly given the military caliber of your kingdom." The rest of the delegation nods assent and pretends amazement with rehearsed gestures of astonishment. The Babylonian committee then is directed to various strategic points of the kingdom. Hezekiah shows them the entirety of the country and its possessions (2 Kgs. 20:13).

Important Questions

While the king continues to show off his riches to his guests, the prophet Isaiah appears. The man of God is now elderly. He detains the king and points with his finger at the foreigners dressed in their bright and elegant clothing. Their garments are embroidered with the pagan symbols of their deities.

"Who are these people and from what place did they come?"

A boastful smile appears on King Hezekiah's face and his voice expresses pride in the honour shown him by the king of Babylon (Isa. 39:1). "These are highly placed ambassadors from Babylon. I have a close relationship with the emperor because I have 'connections.' They know that we have come to be a key nation that can no longer be ignored in international matters."

Unsatisfied, the prophet asks, "What have they seen in your house?"

"They have seen all that is in my house; there is nothing among my treasures that I have not shown them" (Isa. 39:4).

"Hear the word of the LORD of Hosts: 'Behold the days are coming when all that is in your house, and what your fathers have accumulated until this day, shall be carried to Babylon'" (Isa. 39:5-6).

Isaiah continues with a voice like a hammer driving a stake into the ground. *"'Nothing shall be nothing left,' says the LORD. 'And they shall take away some of your sons who will descend from you, whom you will beget; and they shall be eunuchs in the palace of the king of Babylon'"* (Isa. 39:6-7).

Hezekiah grows weak at the knees, and a cold sweat covers his body. He looks as if he is about to faint. At last he recovers and admits his sin. Instead of protesting his innocence, the king humbly acknowledges, *"The word of the LORD which you have spoken is good!"* Then, almost to himself, he says, *"At least there will be peace and truth in my days"* (Isa. 39:8).

Nevertheless, that night Hezekiah could not find sleep. The words of the prophet return to him time and again, and he recollects earlier moments in his life. The great Passover celebration comes to mind: *"Since the time of Solomon the son of David, king of Israel, there had been nothing like this in Jerusalem"* (2 Chron. 30:26). He remembers the multitudes, how they danced in the streets and sang praises to the Lord. He recalls how he offered the sacrifice and the joy that he felt in worshipping God as prescribed in Scripture.

The invasion of Judah by the army of Sennacherib then fills the king's thoughts. He could never forget the insults and threats the Assyrian commander directed at him or how, with anguish and a heavy heart, he walked through the streets and up to the temple. There, in the house of God, Hezekiah spread out the menacing letter before Him and prayed for His salvation. In response God had declared, *"For I will defend this city, to save it for My own sake and for My servant David's sake"* (2 Kgs. 19:8-19, 34).

Sleep still evades the king. His life seems like a movie that won't stop until the final scene is shown.

Hezekiah's mind turns to the illness that he had suffered, how it worsened, and how no one was able to cure him. He recollects how he wept in the presence of God when Isaiah the prophet told him his days were numbered (Isa. 38:1). He remembers the sundial of Ahaz and how the shadow had gone back ten degrees, an impossible occurrence (2 Kgs. 20:8-11).

Hezekiah: The Best of Them?

Finally he vividly recalls, earlier that day, the prophet's words of condemnation, words provoked by Hezekiah's own dealings with the foreign emissaries.

At length, Hezekiah rises from his luxurious bed and humbly kneels down and prays to the Lord. His prayer is long, sincere, and accompanied by many tears. In the dim light we can see his face, now radiant with the peace of God (Phil. 4:7).

The Bible Back-Story

It was during the reign of King Hezekiah that the northern kingdom (i.e. Israel) came to an end following its conquest by the Assyrians.

The temple was purified during the week of the beginning of Hezekiah's reign, suggesting that he had been a co-regent with his father. It's probable that this plan had been laid out many months before the death of the progenitor.

How was it possible that Hezekiah could have accumulated so much wealth after having sent a tribute to the king of Assyria (2 Kgs. 18:15)? A substantial portion could have been obtained from the spoils that were left behind by Sennacharib's army (2 Kgs. 19:35).

The king's fortune was remarkable. *"Hezekiah had very great riches and honour. And he made himself treasuries for silver, for gold, for precious stones, for spices, for shields, and for all kinds of desirable items"* (2 Chron. 32:27). Undoubtedly Hezekiah had been careful to encourage agronomy and livestock production within his kingdom. The biblical text also tells us that he had *"storehouses for the harvest of grain, wine, and oil; and stalls for all kinds of livestock, and folds for flocks"* (2 Chron. 32:28).

In addition to religious reforms and the re-institution of the long-neglected Passover, King Hezekiah is famous for his engineering projects. The most notable of these was the excavation of a tunnel to transport water into Jerusalem from outside the walls of the city, a distance of more than 1700 feet...Hezekiah's tunnel remains to this day. What's more, he *"stopped the water*

outlet of Upper Gihon, and brought the water by tunnel to the west
side of the City of David" (2 Chron. 32:30).

The Struggles in Our Lives

Keep Your Priorities

Hezekiah started well and ended well. He was one of the
best kings in the history of Judah. From the point of view of his
personal life and morality, he never fell into any of the serious
sins that beset many of the other kings of whom the Bible nevertheless declares that they "did that which was right." Neither
did he fall into idolatry, as did Solomon and others, nor commit adultery and murder, as did David. The Bible itself, in fact,
declares that, *"there was none like him among all the kings of Judah"*
(2 Kgs. 18:5).

Hezekiah's priorities were spiritual. His first public act as
governor of the people of Judah was not eliminating his political enemies or reorganizing the army, but repairing and
opening the doors of the house of the Lord. Hezekiah had a
profound love for the temple (Ps. 84:1-2). His entire life can be
characterized by three noteworthy qualities:

- He was faithful to the Lord.
- He did not depart from the Lord.
- He was diligent to keep the commandments of the Lord
  (2 Kgs. 18:6).

Why did this man have such a noble character when his
father was so wicked? Perhaps it is because of his mother.
The Bible refers to her specifically as *"Abijah, the daughter of
Zechariah"* (2 Chron. 29:1). Certainly both Hezekiah's mother
and grandfather had much to do with instilling in the youth the
fear of God.

Take Sin Seriously

Hezekiah's speech to the priests and Levites was both
encouraging and inspiring. He acknowledges that his royal

forerunners, as well as the people themselves, had been guilty of sinning against the Lord. He was well aware that disobedience and rebellion against God bear their consequences. 2,500 years later we have come to believe erroneously that we can live in open sin without concern for God's judgment.

The words Hezekiah employs demonstrate his recognition of the seriousness of the people's actions: *"they have forsaken Him...they have turned their faces away...they have turned their backs on Him"* (2 Chron. 29:6). With equally bold terms he expresses his decision: *"Now it is in my heart to make a covenant with the LORD God of Israel, that His fierce wrath may turn away from us"* (2 Chron. 29:10).

We must ask ourselves whether our society is falling into the same depth of spiritual idolatry as was the case in Hezekiah's time. In our culture many elements of paganism are becoming increasingly acceptable. I personally have seen hundreds of people in South America awaiting the setting of the sun so that they could greet the "Astral King" with enthusiastic applause.

The pantheism of the ancient peoples has subtly infiltrated our society and is being manifested in widespread veneration and personification of nature. Yet even more troubling is the corruption of the gospel (Gal. 1:8) and the preaching of another Jesus and another Spirit (1 Cor. 11:4).

The bronze serpent that Moses had placed on a post had come to be an object of idolatry to the Jewish people (1 Kgs. 18:4). The object had to be destroyed; no compromise was possible. In similar fashion, items of antiquity, that in themselves may have historical religious value, can easily degenerate into idolatrous relics. The Christian is called to worship in spirit and in truth, not to venerate relics.

Perhaps there is a bronze serpent lingering in our lives as well that needs to be destroyed. It may be something that God used in the past to help us mature but has since taken on inordinate significance. Even service to God may become an "idol." The work of the Lord must never become the focus of our lives but rather we should keep our eyes upon our beloved Saviour.

Projects, buildings, programs, and establishing churches can become dangerous "bronze serpents."

Help Bring About Godly Change

Consider the brief spiritual awakening that occurred during the king's reign. The anatomy and physiology characteristic of revivals are seen here.

The doors of the house of the Lord were opened. Not only were the doors opened in a physical sense, but spiritually a revival begins with the doors of the hearts of the people being swung wide open in searching for God (Isa. 55:6).

The doors were repaired. King Hezekiah instilled in the Levites and priests a fervent desire to serve God (2 Chron 29:12-17) and they immediately sought to repair the doors of the temple. Spiritual interest is always manifested by a desire to remove any hindrances to access to God. The doors speak figuratively of separation when closed, but of free and unhindered communication when open.

Hezekiah gathered together the priests and Levites to exhort them. His exhortation was based not only on his position as king, but also on his personal consecration to the Almighty (v 4). His message was to not neglect the things of the Lord and to put God first. Hezekiah first committed himself to do the same and was then able to lead others (2 Tim. 4:1-2).

The priests sanctified themselves. This is a prerequisite for service for the Lord. Centuries later the apostle would reiterate the same principle: *"Therefore, having these promises, beloved, let us cleanse ourselves from all filthiness of the flesh and spirit, perfecting holiness in the fear of God"* (2 Cor. 7:1). Just as the priests and Levites cleansed the house of the Lord, we should let God *"sanctify you completely; and may your whole spirit, soul, and body be preserved blameless at the coming of our Lord Jesus Christ"* (1 Thess. 5:23).

They offered sacrifices to the Lord. Only after have the above steps have been taken can one rightly reverence the Lord. This is true worship.

Hezekiah: The Best of Them?

Return to God

Hezekiah experienced two great trials during his life. On a national level, there was the invasion by Sennacharib. On a personal level, there was the illness that nearly occasioned his death. In each case God worked miraculously and the result was praise to the Lord for His grace and faithfulness. In both of these events Isaiah the prophet played a key role.

Perhaps Hezekiah was motivated by pride when he showed his enemies all his treasures. God roundly condemns this sin (1 Pet. 5:5). Nevertheless, the final fall of Jerusalem was due to Judah's idolatry and the people's abandonment of God. The words of Isaiah the prophet should thus be understood with a sense of irony as if saying, "All that you have shown to them and of which you are so proud, will be taken from you."

If Hezekiah had not shown them his treasures, the result would nevertheless have been the same, although possibly postponed. When Hezekiah heard the sentence uttered by Isaiah, he responds with proper humility. He did not grow angry against the prophet of God but rather accepts his words and says to Isaiah, *"'The word of the LORD which you have spoken is good!' For he said, 'Will there not be peace and truth at least in my days?'"* (2 Kgs. 20:19).

Mathew Poole interprets Hezekiah's answer as saying in effect, "I will submit to this punishment because it is at the same time both a just judgment which I deserve as a result of my own guilt and the guilt of my people and also a merciful judgment because the punishment is less than I deserve."[1]

This is the only serious fault mentioned in the life of this pious family. We read that *"regarding the ambassadors of the princes of Babylon, whom they sent to him to inquire about the wonder that was done in the land, God withdrew from him, in order to test him, that He might know all that was in his heart"* (2 Chron. 32:31).

Surely Hezekiah knew the danger of showing his treasures. Perhaps supreme self-confidence led him to do so, or perhaps it was the hope of gaining an advantage for Judah in a peace treaty with Babylon. J. Barton Payne asserts,

"The basic purpose of the testing of Hezekiah with the emissaries was to determine whether he would trust in human treaties or in God. It was his eagerness to seek treaties that incurred the wrath of the Lord."[2] In this respect we are no different from the king. How easy it is for those in the work of the Lord to trust in their own talents, abilities, and gifts (Gal. 6:3) instead of the strength of the Lord (Phil. 4:13).

We are told something about Hezekiah that is not mentioned about any other king. We read not merely the familiar phase about the good kings of Judah (*"He did what was right in the sight of the LORD"*) but the following: *"he did what was good and right and true before the LORD his God. And in every work that he began in the service of the house of God, in the law and in the commandment, to seek his God, he did it with all his heart"* (2 Chron. 31:20-21).

King Hezekiah is an example to us because of his integrity, faithfulness, and perseverance in the things of God. The result was God's blessing on him.

Using Our Gifts

One challenge that every leader will eventually face is having to act contrary to popular opinion. Doing away with the bronze serpent, an object of great historical value, was certainly a controversial step. But Hezekiah was a man who was more concerned about pleasing God than about pleasing the majority. *"For do I now persuade men, or God? Or do I seek to please men? For if I still pleased men, I would not be a bondservant of Christ"* (Gal 1:10).

The dangers of alliances and associations with "persons in error" are clearly seen in the account of Hezekiah's dealings with Babylon. A leader who joins forces or unites with persons or organizations that are disobedient to the Word of God jeopardizes His divine blessing. One of the greatest kings of Judah stained his testimony by trusting in human strength rather than depending totally upon the Lord.

Hezekiah: The Best of Them?

Discussion Starters

1. How can we encourage the Lord's servants?

2. Is material prosperity, as in the case of Hezekiah, evidence of God's blessing?

3. How do we recognize those who, like the Babylonian emissaries, come with deceitful motives?

4. In what circumstances are you tempted to boast about or show off your possessions, talents, abilities, eloquence, or musical gifts?

Chapter 11

JOSIAH: NOT A CHIP OFF THE OLD BLOCK

"Come quickly! Look what I've found!" exclaims the High Priest. Shaphan the scribe hastens to Hilkiah's side, takes a carefully rolled parchment, and examines it carefully. He respectfully, but excitedly, nods his head.

Buried Treasure

The Book of Books

The two men have discovered nothing less than the long-missing scrolls of the Book of the Law of God. Hilkiah enthusiastically tells Shaphan that they must take the scrolls to the king at once.

The ruler of Judah is a remarkable young man, barely twenty-six years old. The burdens of his position, however, have aged him considerably; he appears older than his years.

Shaphan reports to King Josiah, *"Your servants have gathered the money that was found in the house, and have delivered it into the hand of those who do the work, who oversee the house of the LORD"* (2 Kgs. 22:9).

"Very well," responds Josiah. "Is there anything more to tell me?"

"Yes, my king. Hilkiah the priest has given me some scrolls. He found them hidden in a corner during the search that you had ordered. It is the Book of the Law of the Lord!"

The king is incredulous. "Are you certain? It has been so long since the Book was lost."

"Yes, your majesty. Hilkiah assures me that it is a faithful copy of the Book of the Law."

Josiah reverently takes the ancient scroll in his hands. "I have heard many things about this Book. Often I have thought of what a blessing it would be to see what my ancestors possessed and to hear its words. But enough. Read it at once!"

Shaphan the scribe begins to read. All who are present in the palace courtroom listen with rapt attention. Never in his life has Josiah heard such truths. Naturally, he had been taught aspects of the Scriptures, but what he was now hearing was "from the beginning." After two or three hours the scribe asks, "Your majesty, I have been reading a good while. Would you like to rest and resume later?"

"No! Please continue!"

Verse by verse Shaphan reads the Book of Deuteronomy:

> For the LORD your God is a consuming fire, a jealous God.   Deuteronomy 4:24

> Therefore know that the LORD your God, He is God, the faithful God who keeps covenant and mercy for a thousand generations with those who love Him and keep His commandments.   Deuteronomy 7:9

> The LORD delighted only in your fathers, to love them; and He chose their descendants after them, you above all peoples, as it is this day.
>   Deuteronomy 10:15

Josiah: Not a Chip Off the Old Block

Josiah grows still and quiet. He is absorbed with listening. Then tears form in his eyes and trickle down his cheeks. When Shaphan notices the king's emotional distress, he pauses. Josiah gestures for the scribe to proceed.

> Your fathers went down to Egypt with seventy persons, and now the LORD your God has made you as the stars of heaven in multitude.
>
> Deuteronomy 10:22

> But it shall come to pass, if you do not obey the voice of the LORD your God, to observe carefully all His commandments and His statutes which I command you today, that all these curses will come upon you and overtake you.   Deuteronomy 28:15

> The LORD will strike you with madness and blindness and confusion of heart. And you shall grope at noonday, as a blind man gropes in darkness; you shall not prosper in your ways; you shall be only oppressed and plundered continually, and no one shall save you.   Deuteronomy 28:28-29

> As an eagle stirs up its nest, hovers over its young, spreading out its wings, taking them up, carrying them on its wings, so the LORD alone led him, and there was no foreign god with him.
>
> Deuteronomy 32:11-12

At length Shaphan ends his reading. Long hours have passed since he picked up the first scroll and began to read. Many of those who were present in the royal court have drawn near to better hear the words of the Lord.

Response and Repentance

The ruler seems enveloped by a deep sorrow. An artist, perhaps, could portray the tapestry of emotions that his face reveals. There is sadness, anguish of heart, and anxiety. The king reflects on the grievous sins committed by his people, including his father, Amon, and his grandfather, Manasseh—two kings who *"did evil in the sight of the Lord"* (2 Chron. 33:22).

Josiah arises and tears his garments in repentance. A grimace of anguish covers his face as he falls to his knees and begins to weep profusely. The young king cries out to the Lord for mercy. Some of those present whisper, "What has our nation done that is so wrong? Has he become a religious legalist?"

At length, the king orders, *"Go, inquire of the LORD for me, and for those who are left in Israel and Judah, concerning the words of the book that is found; for great is the wrath of the LORD that is poured out on us, because our fathers have not kept the word of the LORD, to do according to all that is written in this book"* (2 Chron. 34:21).

The person who will reveal the message of God is Huldah the prophetess, whom Hilkiah and others visited. When they return, the king and his court gather to hear God's answer. The first part of the message is directed toward the people: *"Thus says the LORD: 'Behold, I will bring calamity on this place and on its inhabitants, all the curses that are written in the book which they have read before the king of Judah, because they have forsaken Me and burned incense to other gods, that they might provoke Me to anger with all the works of their hands. Therefore My wrath will be poured out on this place, and not be quenched'"* (2 Chron. 34:24-25).

Josiah and his counselors grow pale. The judgment has been pronounced, and there is no way to avoid impending retribution. Judah has passed the point at which the people's sins could go unpunished; catastrophe is imminent (Isa. 55:6). The king anxiously listens to the second part of the message from the prophetess, which is directed to him: *"...'because your heart was tender, and you humbled yourself before God when you heard His words against this place and against its inhabitants, and you humbled yourself before Me, and you tore your clothes and wept before Me, I also have heard you,' says the LORD"* (2 Chron. 34:27).

The king listens carefully. He raises his arms and lifts his eyes heavenward, in gratitude. The message continues, *"Surely I will gather you to your fathers, and you shall be gathered to your grave in peace; and your eyes shall not see all the calamity which I will bring on this place and its inhabitants"* (2 Chron. 34:28).

Josiah falls to the floor weeping. He recognizes that calamity is rapidly approaching. That night he refuses food in order to fast and pray. A few days later he calls for the elders of Judah and Jerusalem and tells them to prepare a great convocation of all the inhabitants of the land, from the greatest to the smallest.

A New Day for Judah

On the day of the assembly, thousands and thousands gather for a time of national repentance and of crying out to the Lord. In the midst of the great court the multitude patiently awaits the appearance of the ruler. Finally he enters, walking slowly with regal dignity. He ascends a platform and looks around at the people.

The Bible tells us, *"The king went up to the house of the LORD, with all the men of Judah and the inhabitants of Jerusalem—the priests and the Levites, and all the people, great and small. And he read in their hearing all the words of the Book of the Covenant which had been found in the house of the LORD"* (2 Chron. 34:30).

When the people hear "the words of the Book," many begin to weep. The little children don't understand what is happening. "Mommy, why is grandfather crying?" asks a young boy. His mother tries to explain, "It is because we have sinned gravely and God is angry with His people."

"Then the king stood by a pillar and made a covenant before the LORD, to follow the LORD and to keep His commandments and His testimonies and His statutes, with all his heart and all his soul, to perform the words of this covenant that were written in this book" (2 Kgs. 23:3).

There is a long silence. Then the response: "And all the people took a stand for the covenant."

An Unforgettable Passover

"The king is a legalist," murmurs a court official discreetly to a younger colleague.

He responds, "You're right! Josiah wants to do everything according to the law of Moses. But times have changed."

The older man adds, "What he wants to do is impossible. The last time the Passover was celebrated was more than one hundred years ago. My grandfather told me what his father related of something similar that King Hezekiah did. They had to postpone the celebration for a month because they were unable to complete the preparations and consecrate enough priests" (2 Chron. 30:3).

"If you ask me, if the king really wants to do this, I think it would be easier to plan it for the third or fourth month. That would give us more time and perhaps the weather would be a bit better."

"The monarch is insistent," responds the other. "He says it must take place on the fourteenth of the first month."

"But if all of Judah and a good part of Israel come to the cele-bration, what will we do? How can we handle so many people? There aren't enough houses for so many even if we included the outlying towns and villages. Where will we find enough food to provide for such a multitude?"

The weeks pass and the older official finds his younger colleague in one of the palace chambers. He again speaks to him, but in different tones. "You know, I'm getting excited about celebrating the Passover. The priests are saying that God promises His blessing on those that obey Him. We have to admit things have gone well since Josiah began to govern the land."

"Have you heard the latest? King Josiah has pledged thirty thousand sheep, lambs, and kids, and also three thousand oxen of his own herds and flocks."

"You mean they were his own property?" asks the older man in disbelief. "His grandfather never gave *anything* to any-*one*. In fact, King Manasseh robbed many people."

"The nobles have also given an enormous quantity of live-stock. The king has ordered the priests to prepare themselves. The gatekeepers are to be present and in place."

Josiah: Not a Chip Off the Old Block

Outside the palace walls children play and shout to one another, "We are going to have a great party! We're going to celebrate the Passover of the Lord!"

A young boy walking home with his father overhears the others and asks, "Daddy, what is the Passover?" The father carefully recounts the story of the death of all the firstborn of Egypt, of the blood of the lamb sprinkled on the doorposts of the Jewish people, and of their deliverance from slavery.

At last the long-anticipated day arrives. An immense sense of joy pervades Jerusalem. The villages surrounding the great capital of Judah are filled with hundreds of visitors, the overflow from the city itself. On that day, from the most poor and humble to the nobles of the royal palace, the feeling of anticipation is the same. Each family celebrates the Passover with great gladness and joy and the Lord fills the nation with His peace.

The same child says to his father, "Daddy, how wonderful the Passover is. I want to have another one!"

Honest but Unwise?

The Egyptian Threat

The grand hall of the royal palace was resplendent with the glowing lights of countless oil lamps. The king has convened a session of his ministers and his chief commanders. The highest religious authorities are in attendance as well. Thirteen years of relative peace have passed since the great celebration of the Passover. During these years Josiah has sought diligently to increase his military strength and to maintain a strong defensive posture.

"My esteemed ministers of cabinet, generals, and servants of the Lord," the king begins, "the reason I have called you together with such urgency is that we have been notified by certain sources that Pharaoh Necho is marching toward our land with an extraordinarily powerful army. Egypt is a mighty empire and we are but a small nation. We are mindful, however, that God is on our side and that He is all-powerful. Now, tell me your suggestions and advice concerning the situation that confronts us."

The commander-in-chief of the army rises first. His face reveals the steadfastness and determination that has brought him successfully through many years of hard military campaigning and combat. "Your Majesty, our army is ready and willing to defend our nation's soil. We left behind our slavery in Egypt when Moses led us forth from that nation of bondage and we will not again return to servitude. I swear that we will fight to the last man. If we let the enemy army enter our land and become entrenched here, there will be no possible way to later expel him."

The second in command stands up. With a strong voice he affirms, "Your Highness, I am in agreement with what the commander has said. But the truth is, we do not have the military capability to directly confront the Egyptians. They have a professional army. They possess chariots and sophisticated weapons of war. There is no way or manner by which we may challenge them and defeat them. Nevertheless, it is as Your Highness has said, if God be with us they will never defeat us."

Anxious murmurs resonate through the room.

A ministerial official—elderly, a bit heavy-set, balding, and with smallish eyes that dart back and forth—is the next to speak. "My King, I am very patriotic, but a dead patriot serves no purpose. I believe that we must immediately send an emissary to the Pharaoh and declare to him that we are willing not only to let him pass through our territory but also to provide him with all he needs. We need to formalize a treaty of non-aggression and offer our cooperation, with funds for any purposes that the pharaoh has in mind."

One by one the others stand and voice their support for a policy of non-aggression.

King Josiah takes the floor. He is thirty-nine years old but retains all the vigor and strength of his youth. With confidence and determination, he addresses those assembled before him. "Priests, ministers, and generals. My great-grandfather King

Josiah: Not a Chip Off the Old Block

Hezekiah once was surrounded by an enormous army of 185,000 soldiers under the command of the Assyrian general, Sennacherib. Jerusalem was as good as lost.

"But my great-grandfather prayed to the Lord and committed the cause to Him. The prophet Isaiah joined him in this earnest supplication. You know the story well: God sent His Angel and in a single night shattered the enemy army.

"As ruler of this people, I am obligated to defend our nation. We simply cannot permit this enormous army to invade our lands. We must not allow them to cross our territory. As a descendant of King David I decree that the army of Judah prepare itself to do battle against the enemy. May the Lord's will be done!"

A gloomy silence descends on the room, as if the chill of death itself can be felt. At last one of the ministers exclaims with a shout, "Long live King Josiah!"

Suddenly all the men raise their arms and shout in support of the king's resolve. Then, once again, silence slowly envelopes the assembly.

Troops Are Deployed

Several weeks pass during which the troops under the command of Josiah deploy themselves along the frontier in order to block the passage of the Egyptian army. At the command post on the front lines, an emergency meeting is convened. In the campaign tent the king stands with his army chiefs. A herald from the Egyptian army has just arrived with a message from Pharaoh Necho himself. The envoy is brought into the presence of the monarch, to whom he respectfully bows.

"I bear a message for the king," begins the herald. "Thus says Pharaoh Necho, *'What have I to do with you, King of Judah? I have not come against you this day, but against the house with which I have war; for God commanded me to make haste. Refrain from meddling with God, who is with me, lest He destroy you'*" (2 Chron. 35:21).

The courier awaits Josiah's response, which is immediate: "Tell your master that I am prepared to defend my nation unto the last man."

The Egyptian herald bows and withdraws.

"Your Majesty," declares the commander-in-chief, "We are willing to follow you to death if it be necessary."

The second in command says, "Your Highness, I am as ready as anyone to lay down my life for His Majesty and for Judah. But I wonder if it might be more sensible to attempt to avoid conflict, at least for the moment. After all, Pharaoh Necho has assured us that he is not seeking to fight against us. Perhaps he is telling the truth."

Another ventures to speak, "My King, the pharaoh says that he is rushing to battle because God has told him to make haste. Could it be that the God of Israel is now acting on behalf of the king of Egypt?"

Josiah becomes livid but eventually regains his composure and exclaims, "Our enemies always say that God is on their side. It is their way to discourage us. And I cannot believe that God would support an idolatrous ruler, a blasphemer and a mocker."

The ruler deftly unsheathes his sword and raises its glistening blade. "As king of Judah my duty is to defend our land. We will fight against Pharaoh Necho!"

Death of a Soldier-King

A few days later the battle is enjoined. The generals and commanders insist that Josiah not enter the battlefield in his royal chariot or dress in regal garments.

The king reluctantly accedes to his officers' request. He goes forth to battle clothed as a common soldier. Nevertheless, the enemy recognizes that one of the attacking chariots is being driven by a man of undoubted importance. With courage and fearlessness King Josiah is leading his army.[1]

Hundreds of arrows streak through the air toward Josiah. The king staggers in his chariot as he shouts, *"Take me away, for I am severely wounded"* (2 Chron. 35:23). As the arrows continue to fly, the royal servants pull Josiah into their own chariot and race away from the battlefield to Jerusalem. As the king lies quietly on the bouncing floor of the chariot, he remembers God's words: *"Surely, therefore, I will gather you to your fathers, and you shall be gathered to your grave in peace"* (2 Kgs. 22:20a). A vague smile appears on the face of the dying king as he slowly turns his gaze heavenward.

The Bible Back-Story

The Great Discovery

Shaphan the scribe served as the secretary of the king (2 Kgs. 22:8). It would seem that he was a godly man. His influence would be felt not only during his own life but also through the lives of his sons— Ahikam (Jer. 26:24), Elasah (Jer. 29:3), and Gemariah (Jer 36:25)—and his grandson Gedaliah (Jer. 39:14).[2]

The portion of the Book of the Law that was discovered was probably the Book of Deuteronomy or sections thereof, particularly chapters 28 and 30. Josiah was concerned about the spiritual state of affairs, not only of Judah but also of the kingdom of Israel (the northern kingdom), as seen in 2 Chronicles 34:21.

We may wonder why Josiah didn't consult with well-known prophets of that time, Zephaniah, Jeremiah, or Nahum. It is felt by many that Zephaniah would have still been very young. Jeremiah and Nahum may have been out of the city. Nevertheless, Huldah the prophetess was held in high regard by the Jewish writers. She and Jehoida the priest are the only persons who, although not being of the house of David, are specifically mentioned as being buried in Jerusalem (2 Chron. 24:16).

The tearing or rending of one's vestments, such as King Josiah did, was a sign of deep sadness, mourning, or even indignation toward blasphemy (Matt. 26:65; Acts 14:14).

Reign of Reform

The Passover celebration in the days of Josiah took place around the year 622 BC. Approximately 37,600 sheep were sacrificed. If it is assumed that one sheep was offered per ten persons, then around 376,000 people attended the Passover.[3]

The great majority of the inhabitants of the Northern Kingdom (Israel) were in exile at the time of Josiah's reign. Nevertheless those remaining were among the ones who joyously made the journey to Jerusalem.

Josiah is one of the few kings mentioned in Scripture who brought about a spiritual revival. He would live for only thirteen more years, but the influence of his dedicated spiritual leadership endured far beyond his death.

Battle Lessons

The Egyptian army had sallied forth to support the Syrian troops, not to fight against them, as some translations indicate. Their combined forces battled the rising Babylonian empire headed by its brilliant chief Nebuchadnezzar. The resulting battle of Carchemish (605 BC) resulted in defeat for Egypt.

Did Josiah do wrong in going to battle? It would seem that with the level of understanding that Josiah possessed at the time he did the right thing. The king was a man who was willing to give his life for his country. "Josiah considered it to be his duty to resist the hostile army that was threatening to enter his territory".[4]

The argument that Pharaoh would not have attacked Judah is incorrect. Returning from the campaign which resulted in his defeat, Necho sent his army against Jerusalem. He removed the son of Josiah from the throne and took him captive. In his place, Necho placed a brother who pledged loyalty to Egypt. In addition, Necho imposed a heavy tax on the land (2 Chron. 36:2). Everyone was now forced to pay tribute to Pharaoh (2 Kgs. 23:35).

Did Josiah sin by disguising himself before venturing onto the battlefield? It must first be recognized that the translation of this passage is somewhat in question. Experts note that the Hebrew word translated as "disguise" can also mean "to strengthen oneself or to encourage oneself for battle"[5] or "to equip oneself".[6]

However, even if we allow that Josiah may have disguised his identity during the battle, it would be wise not to judge him inordinately for having done so. The fact that Josiah himself sought to attack Necho seems to contradict the idea that the king was occupied only with his own well-being. "Although disguised, the king appeared to the enemy to be at least a general, perhaps the commander in chief, and therefore they attacked him.[7]

The Death of Josiah

Nineveh and the Assyrian empire fell in 612 BC, three years before King Josiah's death in the year 609 BC.[8]

The prophetess Huldah had indicated to Josiah that he would be *"gathered to his fathers in peace"* (2 Chron. 34:28). In effect, this was a promise that he would be properly buried and not an indication of the way he would die. A honourable internment was a matter of great importance in Jewish tradition. The phrase "gathered to his fathers" is one of many in the Old Testament that affirm life after death (Job 19:25; 1 Sam. 28:19).

Finally, there is an apparent discrepancy as to where Josiah actually died. The account in 2 Kings (23:29) indicates that he was killed in Meggido, while 2 Chronicles (35:24) seems to specify Jerusalem as the place of the king's demise. The solution to the dilemma is that while Josiah was mortally wounded in Megiddo, he most likely actually died while being taken to Jerusalem.

The Struggles in Our Lives

Focus on What You Have

"A chip off the old block." We've heard the phrase many times and it often is true. So it is that we are particularly saddened to hear about the child of a famous preacher or missionary who has not followed in the parent's footsteps but rather has fallen into serious sin. Yet there are also encouraging stories of precisely the opposite occurring. Such was the case with Josiah.

If home environment and genetics were the only factors, Josiah would have been a lost cause. His father was the wicked Amon, who reigned for only two years yet led Judah deep into idolatry. About him we read, *"So he walked in all the ways that his father had walked; and he served the idols that his father had served, and worshiped them"* (2 Kgs. 21:21).

Josiah's grandfather Manasseh (who died when Josiah was only six years old) was another terribly wicked king. In contrast with that of Amon, Manasseh's reign was very long, fifty-five years, during which iniquity flourished in the nation to an astonishing extent. The Bible characterizes Manasseh by the multitude of crimes committed against the faithful who opposed his pagan practices. Moreover Manasseh shed very much innocent blood, till he had filled Jerusalem from one end to another (2 Kgs. 21:16).

How then is it possible that such a pious and God-fearing man as Josiah could appear on the scene under such dispiriting circumstances? Many of the great men and women of God have arisen during times of intense spiritual darkness. The Almighty, in His providence, works in wonderful ways. Perhaps some of Josiah's relatives taught him to fear God. Many believe that Josiah's spiritual hunger was nurtured by the prophet Zephaniah (635-625 BC). Regardless of the means, the Lord put a wall of protection around the young prince; consequently, he became one of the most devout kings in the history of Judah.

Christians can be tempted to lament what we do not have, be it talents, possessions, or family background. The Scriptures, however, encourage us: *"we are more than conquerors"* (Rom. 8:37); *"I can do all things through Christ who strengthens me"* (Phil. 3:13); *"Greater is He that is within you than he that is in the world"* (1 John 4:4).

Stay on a Fixed Course

Notice how the Scriptures introduce Josiah. When Josiah was sixteen years old he began to seek the God of his father David (2 Chron. 34:3). The sacred writer, guided by the Holy Spirit, relates the boy king not to his earthly father Amon but to his godly ancestor David. Josiah, by birth a rich prince, came to be not only king but a servant of God. David, a poor shepherd in his youth, likewise came to be not merely a ruler but a servant of God.

Josiah: Not a Chip Off the Old Block

The life of Josiah can be summarized by the phrase *"And he did what was right in the sight of the LORD, and walked in the ways of his father David; he did not turn aside to the right hand or to the left"* (2 Chron. 34:2). This expression, used several times in the Scriptures, should not be construed to mean that the individuals were without fault or never erred. Still, when God views their entire lives, He summarizes their goals and lifestyles with profound words of commendation (Luke 12:37-38). How wonderful if God were able to say the same of us!

What did Josiah do to not deviate either to the left or to the right? Any navigator would affirm that, to stay on a fixed course, one needs a compass or a way point, a goal, something that he can look toward. In today's world we would say that we need a global positioning system. The author of the Letter to the Hebrews reveals the spiritual equivalent when he urges us to look *"unto Jesus, the author and finisher of our faith"* (Heb. 12:2).

Fulfil Your Calling

Some men are remembered for their great military victories. Others, such as Solomon, are memorialized by undertaking magnificent architectural wonders. Josiah, however, comes by his "page of fame" by being the instrument by whom God initiated a spiritual revival among His people. We read the words of approval found in the Scriptures: *"There had been no Passover kept in Israel like that since the days of Samuel the prophet"* (2 Chron 35:18). When God Himself gives His stamp of approval, who can say anything more?

King Josiah likely was called a legalist by many. The term **legalism** is defined by Webster as a "strict, literal, or excessive conformity to the law or to a religious code." Josiah was not a legalist in the derogatory sense; he was a sincere believer who sought to be faithful to what the Scriptures taught. The Lord Jesus consistently maintained a similar attitude (John 4:34). The church needs more men and women like Josiah today!

Today we often hear, "times have changed." It can be used to downplay biblical truths and practices that are no longer appealing to prevailing practices. Yet the Gospel's message for today is just the same as it was two thousand years ago and should always be presented with equal simplicity and purity (Rom. 1:16; 1 Tim. 1:15).

In Josiah's day, the Ark of the Covenant held a very important place as the focus of worship in the Temple. Similarly, in our churches, the person of Jesus Christ must always have first place in our devotion and worship. Josiah sought to assiduously follow the Scriptures that existed at that time; we too must revere the Holy Bible as the authority that it is.

The Passover had as its objective the remembrance of Israel's bondage in Egypt, and liberation by Moses, but perhaps most importantly, the protection conferred upon the Jews by the blood of the lamb. In the same way we should remember the work of the Lamb of God who took away the sins of the world. In the Lord's Supper believers have the opportunity to meditate specifically on His work and obey His command, *"Do this in remembrance of Me"* (1 Cor. 11:24-25).

Trust God in Crises

Was Josiah out of the will of the Lord when he went out to fight against Pharaoh and, as a result, was killed on the field of battle? My view is that he was not; God fulfilled his promise to Josiah by permitting him to die and be buried in peace (prior to the destruction of Judah). This view implies, of course, that God in His providence knew beforehand what Josiah would choose to do.

Josiah was not unaware of the enemy army's vastly superior numbers. Nevertheless the valiant king realized that the only logical alternative was to defend the homeland, and he was fully prepared to assume the dangerous position of leading his army against them. There is a certain similarity between Josiah's attitude and that of Paul's when the latter responded to the "negative" prophecy of Agabus by saying: *"For I am ready not only to be bound, but also to die at Jerusalem for the name of the Lord Jesus"* (Acts 21:13b).

Why did God allow a man who had served Him so faithfully die in such a violent manner? Had He abandoned Josiah?

Josiah: Not a Chip Off the Old Block

In Acts 12, James is put to death by Herod. In that same chapter, however, we read that the Lord sent His angel to open the prison doors for Peter. As a consequence, Peter, who was scheduled to be executed the following morning, was saved (Acts 12:1-11). On the one hand the Lord marvelously rescued one of His servants from death by the intervention of an angel; on the other, He permitted the execution of another faithful servant.

The Lord has a unique, purpose for each of us. On occasion a preacher or a missionary who has been a great blessing to the people of God will die suddenly in an accident. We ask ourselves, why does the Lord permit such a thing? The best answer is to be found in the words of Paul: *"Oh the depth of the riches both of the wisdom and knowledge of God! How unsearchable are His judgments and His ways past finding out!"* (Rom. 11:33). To this may be added the consoling thought of the psalmist: *"Precious in the sight of the Lord is the death of His saints"* (Ps. 116:15).

God has not promised to always protect us from adversity, whether it be physical or mental. There are matters of greater importance.

Using Our Gifts

The Bible of a godly leader must be not only in the bookcase or on the nightstand but also in his or her heart. The leader studies it faithfully and also follows its teachings. Like Josiah, a godly leader not only hears God's message but shares it with others.

Notice that, when he convenes the people, King Josiah stands erect next to the pillar—a significant symbol. You and I are not royalty; nevertheless we can be firm pillars in the local church, faithful and unswerving in our service to God (Rev. 3:12).

Josiah demonstrated outstanding spiritual leadership. With his guidance and direction, he *"made all who were present in Israel diligently serve the LORD their God. All his days they did not depart from following the LORD God of their fathers"* (2 Chron. 34:33b). Very few people indeed have had such ability to inspire or have possessed such a contagious spirituality which exhorted and revived the nation. *"And he set the priests* in their duties and encouraged them for the service of the house of the LORD" (2 Chron. 35:2).

As a young man of only twenty-six, he courageously instituted spiritual changes even at the national level, and these bold efforts had received the approval of God. The history of the church abounds with examples of men and women who, from an early age, had an impact on their place and time in history. The Lord through the Holy Spirit can repeat the same blessing in our own place and time through us—if we are wholly given to Him (Eph. 3:20-21).

Many times a leader is confronted with a very difficult decision, perhaps with only a few hours to choose a course of action that will be debated for years. Josiah had to decide between his moral obligation to defend his land and the seemingly hopeless cause of battling a military superpower. He sought God's will and direction; if he decided in error, he nevertheless was honest in his pursuit of God.

Discussion Starters

1. What obstacles did Josiah overcome in order to serve the Lord with all his heart, even from an early age?

2. What results from being faithful to the Scriptures? (See also John 14:21.)

3. In what ways are you a light in a dark world and a pillar in your local church?

4. What are some contemporary examples of tenacity and faithfulness to the Lord in the midst of difficulties?

5. How can we better seek and recognize the will of God?

Chapter 12

CONCLUSION: WHO IS ON THE THRONE?

We have walked a long path through many years of history.

On this journey we have contemplated the lives of many kings, some of whom—such as David and Solomon—are well known. Others have been nearly forgotten; they produced neither great achievements nor glaring failures. The Scriptures simply yet profoundly state that they *"did what was right in the sight of the LORD"* (2 Kgs. 18:3; 2 Chron. 25:2; 29:2; etc.).

The nation of Judah was blessed with several kings who sought to follow God, as well as many who were evil and ungodly. In the nation known as Israel, resulting from the division after the death of Solomon—there was, sadly, not a single king who sought after the Lord.

In the list of kings found in the Scriptures there are a few about which we know very little. Names such as Abijah (2 Chron. 13:1-22) and Jehoahaz (2 Chron. 36:1-3) intrigue us. It is not noted whether these men were good or bad; the final verdict is simply not given. We must assume that there is a good reason why this information is not provided.

Our study of these monarchs has revealed many contrasts. Some either died young or their reigns were brief. Other men had long and fruitful careers. Some of those who did right had fathers who were God-fearing. Others were like a beautiful flower growing in a dirty and unkempt place. They arise out of a background of idolatry and, by the grace of God, they turn to Him with all their heart. Nevertheless, at the end of their lives, each was given the precious divine stamp of approval of having done right.

No one has led a perfect life except the One who is the King of kings and Lord of lords (Rev. 19:16). Indeed, even these "good" kings sinned and fell into familiar traps such as:

- reliance on self rather than God;
- adultery;
- pride;
- worship of idols;
- failure to crush completely the worship of idols;

As the lives of each of these men concluded and one by one they passed from this world, they left behind their crowns. Those who were heirs to the throne were crowned in their places. You and I have not yet received our promised crowns, but the Scriptures emphatically assure us that we are the children of God and kings (John 1:12; Rev. 5:10).

The exhortation of Jesus Christ is bold: *"Behold, I am coming quickly! Hold fast what you have, that no one may take your crown"* (Rev. 3:11).

Footnotes

Chapter One

1. Flavius Josephus, *The Works of Josephus: The Antiquities of the Jews, Book 6* trans. William Whiston (Peabody: Hendrickson Publishers, Inc., 2001), ch. 9, para. 5, pg.166.

2. Ibid., ch. 9, para. 1, pg. 164.

Chapter Two

1. Richad H. Beal, "The Hittites After the Empire Fall"article in *The Expositors Bible Commentary, Volume 3* (Grand Rapids: Zondervan, 1988), 930.

2. Matthew Henry, *Matthew Henry's Commentary , Volume 2, Joshua to Esther* (United States of America: Hendrickson Publishers, Inc., 1991), 392.

3. H. L. Rossier, *Meditations on The Second Book of Samuel* (Sunbury: Believers Bookshelf Inc., 1994) 76.

4. Arthur Pink, *The Life of David* (Ada: Baker Publishing Group, 1981), 16.

Chapter Three

1. Frank E. Gaebelein, *The Expositor's Bible Commentary, Volume 3* (Grand Rapids: Zondervan, 1988), 1098.

2. John Gill, *John Gill's Exposition, Volume 2* (Streamwood:

Primitive Baptist Library, 1979), 665

3. Matthew Henry, *Matthew Henry's Commentary*, *Volume 2*, *Joshua to Esther* (United States of America: Hendrickson Publishers, Inc., 1991), 447.

4. Donald Guthrie, *The New Bible Commentary* (Grand Rapids: InterVarsity Press, 1984), 314

Chapter Four

1. Frank E. Gaebelein, *The Expositor's Bible Commentary*, *Volume 4* (Grand Rapids: Zondervan, 1988), 101.

2. Robert Jamiesson, A. R. Fausset and David Brown, *Jamieson-Fausset-Brown Bible Commentary, Volume 1* (Peabody: Hendrickson Publishers, Inc., 2002) 323

Chapter Five

1. Franz Delitzsch, Carl Friedrich Keil, *Keil & Delitzsch Commentary on the Old Testament, Volume 3* (Peabody: Hendrickson Publishers, Inc., 2006), 32

2. Matthew Henry, *Matthew Henry's Commentary*, *Volume 2*, *Joshua to Esther* (United States of America: Hendrickson Publishers, Inc., 1991), 465.

Chapter Six

1. Frank E. Gaebelein, *The Expositor's Bible Commentary*, *Volume 4* (Grand Rapids: Zondervan, 1988), 486.

2. Robert Jamiesson, A. R. Fausset and David Brown, *Jamieson-Fausset-Brown Bible Commentary, Volume 1* (Peabody: Hendrickson Publishers, Inc., 2002), 537.

3. Ibid., 537.

Footnotes

Chapter Seven

1. Matthew Henry, *Matthew Henry's Commentary*, *Volume 2, Joshua to Esther* (United States of America: Hendrickson Publishers, Inc., 1991), 749.

2. Mathew Poole, *Matthew Poole's Commentary on the Holy Bible, Volume 1* (Peabody: Hendrickson Publishers, Inc., 2008), 842.

3. Franz Delitzsch, Carl Friedrich Keil, *Keil & Delitzsch Commentary on the Old Testament, Volume 3* (Peabody: Hendrickson Publishers, Inc., 2006), 640

1. Frank E. Gaebelein, *The Expositor's Bible Commentary, Volume 4* (Grand Rapids: Zondervan, 1988), 468.

Chapter Eight

1. John F. Walvoord, Roy B. Zuck, *The Bible Knowledge Commentary, Old Testament* (Wheaton, David C. Cook, 1985), 638.

2. Matthew Henry, *Matthew Henry's Commentary*, *Volume 2, Joshua to Esther* (United States of America: Hendrickson Publishers, Inc., 1991), 761

3. Frank E. Gaebelein, *The Expositor's Bible Commentary, Volume 4* (Grand Rapids: Zondervan, 1988), 512

4. Matthew Henry, *Matthew Henry's Commentary*, *Volume 2, Joshua to Esther* (United States of America: Hendrickson Publishers, Inc., 1991), 760

Chapter Nine

1. Herbert Lockyer, *All the Kings and Queens of the Bible* (Grand Rapids: Zondervan, 1961) 129.

2. H.L. Rossier, *Meditations on The Second Book of Chronicles* (Sunbury: Believers Bookshelf Inc., 1993) 116.

3. Flavius Josephus, *The Works of Josephus: The Antiquities of the Jews, Book 9* trans. William Whiston (Peabody: Hendrickson Publishers, Inc., 2001), ch. 10, para. 4, pg. 260.

Chapter Ten

1. Mathew Poole, *Matthew Poole's Commentary on the Holy Bible, Volume 1* (Peabody: Hendrickson Publishers, Inc., 2008), 763.

2. Frank E. Gaebelein, *The Expositor's Bible Commentary, Volume 4* (Grand Rapids: Zondervan, 1988), 542.

Chapter Eleven

1. Flavius Josephus, *The Works of Josephus: The Antiquities of the Jews, Book 10* trans. William Whiston (Peabody: Hendrickson Publishers, Inc., 2001), ch. 5, para. 1, pg. 271.

2. Frank E. Gaebelein, *The Expositor's Bible Commentary, Volume 4* (Grand Rapids: Zondervan, 1988), 282

3. Robert Jamiesson, A. R. Fausset and David Brown, *Jamieson-Fausset-Brown Bible Commentary, Volume 1* (Peabody: Hendrickson Publishers, Inc., 2002), 576

4. Albert Barnes, *Barnes' Notes on the Old Testament, Volume 2* (Ada: Baker Publishing Group, 2001), 303.

5. Robert Jamiesson, A. R. Fausset and David Brown, *Jamieson-Fausset-Brown Bible Commentary, Volume 1* (Peabody: Hendrickson Publishers, Inc., 2002), 577

6. Albert Barnes, *Barnes' Notes on the Old Testament, Volume 2* (Ada: Baker Publishing Group, 2001), 430.

7. John Gill, *John Gill's Exposition, Volume 3* (Streamwood: Primitive Baptist Library, 1979), 101

8. Frank E. Gaebelein, *The Expositor's Bible Commentary, Volume 4* (Grand Rapids: Zondervan, 1988), 554.